Angola and the River Congo

Joachim John Monteiro

Alpha Editions

This edition published in 2024

ISBN : 9789367245484

Design and Setting By
Alpha Editions
www.alphaedis.com
Email - info@alphaedis.com

As per information held with us this book is in Public Domain. This book is a reproduction of an important historical work. Alpha Editions uses the best technology to reproduce historical work in the same manner it was first published to preserve its original nature. Any marks or number seen are left intentionally to preserve its true form.

Contents

(VOLUME 1)...- 1 -
PREFACE. ....- 3 -
CHAPTER I. HISTORY...- 4 -
CHAPTER II. PHYSICAL GEOGRAPHY—CHARACTER OF VEGETATION—RIVERS...- 13 -
CHAPTER III. THE RIVER CONGO A BOUNDARY—SLAVE TRADE—SLAVERY—ORDEAL BY POISON—INSENSIBILITY OF THE NEGRO—INGRATITUDE. ....- 25 -
CHAPTER IV. THE RIVER CONGO—BANANA—PORTO DA LENHA—BOMA—MUSSURONGO TRIBE—PIRATES—MUSHICONGO TRIBE—FISH—PALM CHOP—PALM WINE. ....- 37 -
CHAPTER V. COUNTRY FROM THE RIVER CONGO TO AMBRIZ—VEGETATION—TRADING—CIVILIZATION—COMMERCE—PRODUCTS—IVORY—MUSSERRA—SLEEP DISEASE—SALT—MINERAL PITCH. ....- 45 -
CHAPTER VI. AMBRIZ—TRADE—MALACHITE—ROAD TO BEMBE—TRAVELLING—MOSQUITOES—QUIBALLA TO QUILUMBO—QUILUMBO TO BEMBE. ....- 67 -
CHAPTER VII. BEMBE—MALACHITE DEPOSIT—ROOT PARASITE—ENGONGUI—MORTALITY OF CATTLE—FAIRS—KING OF CONGO—RECEPTIONS—CUSTOMS—SAN SALVADOR—FEVERS—RETURN TO AMBRIZ. ......- 84 -
CHAPTER VIII. CHARACTER OF THE NEGRO—FETISH—CUSTOMS—ARMS AND WAR—DRESS—ZOMBO TRIBE—BURIAL—INSANITY..- 105 -
CHAPTER IX. CUSTOMS OF THE MUSSURONGO, AMBRIZ, AND MUSHICONGO NEGROES—MANDIOCA PLANT—ITS PREPARATIONS—CHILI PEPPER—BANANAS—RATS—WHITE ANT—NATIVE BEER—STRANGE SOUNDS......- 121 -

(VOLUME 1)

PREFACE.

The following description of the country between the River Zaire or Congo, and Mossamedes or Little Fish Bay, comprising ten degrees of latitude, is the result of many years of travel in and exploration of that part of the coast.

My aim has been to present an accurate and truthful account of its more striking features and productions, and of the manners and customs of the various tribes which inhabit it.

I have avoided mentioning more names of places and persons than are necessary, as they would be of little or no interest to the general reader. I have also omitted detailed lists and descriptions of plants and animals that I have collected, as such would only interest naturalists, who are referred to the different scientific publications in which they have been described.

This being the first detailed account of a most interesting and rich part of Tropical Africa, I leave it with confidence to the indulgence of my readers, assuring them that at all events a want of truth is not included in its shortcomings.

CHAPTER I.
HISTORY.

The following sketch of the discovery and earlier history of Angola is translated and condensed from an interesting work in Portuguese by Feo Cardozo, on the 'History of the Governors of Angola' (Paris, 8vo, 1825):—

"The Portuguese, engrossed by the great hopes raised by the conquest of Brazil and the Indies, did not determine to establish themselves in Angola till eighty-four years after they had discovered it. The King of Angola, jealous of the advantages that he supposed his neighbour the King of Congo derived from his trade and intercourse with the Portuguese, determined to send several of his subjects to Portugal to beg the like friendship for himself. Queen Catherine, acceding to his request, sent to him Paulo Diaz de Novaes, grandson of the famous Bartolomeo Diaz, who had discovered the greater part of the West Coast and the Cape of Good Hope. Paulo Diaz left Lisbon in September, 1559, with three ships, a few soldiers, and a present for the King, bearing instructions to open commercial relations with the latter, and to convert him to Christianity. After many dangers he arrived in May, 1560, at the mouth of the River Quanza; the King of Angola was dead, but his son, who then reigned, renewed on his arrival his father's request for friendly relations with the Portuguese. Paulo Diaz, relying on his statements, landed with only twenty men, and leaving the rest on board the ships ordered them to return to Portugal if within a certain time he should not come back to them. He immediately marched to the Court of Angola, where he and his present were received by the King with acclamation.

"After the lapse of a few days, Paulo Diaz, wishing to retire to his ships, was prevented by the King under the pretence of his aid being required in some wars he was then engaged in. He was thus detained a prisoner until the King, hard pressed by the revolt of one of his powerful vassals, determined to allow him to return to Portugal, so that he might bring him assistance. From the missals, altar-stones, and old-fashioned church furniture that he saw in the hands of the negroes during his expedition into the interior, Paulo Diaz concluded that missionaries had already been in the country many years before. Returning to Portugal he gave an account of what he had seen to the King, Dom Sebastian, who sent him back with the title of Conqueror, Coloniser, and Governor of Angola, and conceded to him ample powers for the establishment of the new colony.

"Paulo Diaz left Lisbon in October, 1574, with a fleet of seven ships, and seven hundred men, and sighted land after a passage of three months and a half. Landing on the island facing the present city of Loanda, he took formal possession of it in the name of the King of Portugal. An immense number of negroes witnessed the ceremony, as well as forty Portuguese who had retired from the kingdom of Congo, owing to the wars amongst the negroes of that country.

"The King of Angola received the Portuguese with great joy, and in return for the presents that Dom Sebastian had sent him, gave Paulo Diaz several armlets of silver and of copper, and sticks of Quicongo wood; the silver of the armlets was afterwards made into a chalice and presented to the church of Belem at Lisbon.

"Finding that the island was not suitable for establishing the new colony, the Portuguese removed to the mainland, and choosing the spot now occupied by the fortress of San Miguel, built a church and founded their first colony in Angola. They then aided the King, and enabled him speedily to reduce his rebel vassal to obedience. After several months passed in the greatest friendship, the King of Congo attempted to intrigue against the Portuguese, but without success. Perfect peace existed between the Portuguese and the blacks of Angola for six years, when it was destroyed by the base perfidy of a Portuguese, who begged the King to make him his slave, as he wished to disclose a most important secret. Astonished at this proposition, the King called together his 'Macotas' or council, and in their presence ordered the infamous traitor to divulge it; on which he said that Paulo Diaz planned despoiling him of his kingdom and mines, for which purpose he had collected great stores of powder and ball. Next day the King caused all the Portuguese to appear before him, and in their presence the traitor repeated his story. The Portuguese, in astonishment, attempted to refute the calumny, but without attending to their explanations the King ordered them from his presence, and taking counsel of his 'Macotas' was persuaded by them to destroy at once all the Portuguese, and thus avert the threatened danger. Approving their advice, he feigned forgetfulness of the occurrence, then under pretence of a war in the interior, sent forward the Portuguese, who, ignorant of the stratagem, were all suddenly set upon and murdered, together with the Christian slaves, numbering over a thousand. A similar fate befell all the Portuguese engaged in trading in different parts of the country, and their goods and property were taken possession of. The traitor received the just punishment of his infamy, for the King ordered him to be executed, saying, it was not right that one should live who had caused the death of his countrymen. This cruel butchery concluded, the King sent Paulo Diaz, who was on his journey from Loanda, an order not to proceed beyond the spot at which he should receive it.

"The Governor, though totally ignorant of the horrible catastrophe, distrusted the message, and, retiring to Anzelle, erected a wooden intrenchment, and fortifying it with two small cannon, awaited the solution of the affair. But few days had elapsed before he received tidings of the dreadful tragedy, and of the advance of a great army of blacks to annihilate him and the remaining Portuguese. This news, far from terrifying him, inspired him with the hope of speedily avenging the murder of his countrymen. Animating his garrison, of only 150 men, with the same sentiment, he, with the aid of their two guns, repelled the attack of the blacks, causing such havoc among them that they were completely routed and dispersed; he also sent his lieutenant into the interior to ravage it with fire and sword. This was accomplished so successfully, that the King, repenting of his barbarity, turned against the Macotas who had counselled him, and ordered them all to be put to death.

"Paulo Diaz being reinforced from Portugal, defeated several of the 'Sobas,' or chiefs of Quissama, who attempted to impede his navigation of the River Quanza, defeated a second time the King of Angola, and conquered the greater part of the Provinces of Quissama and Illamba, the whole of which he could not occupy from want of men. He then, resolving to acquire the silver mines said to exist in the mountains of Cambambe, fortified himself with his Lieutenant, Luis Serrão, and 120 men, at Tacandongo, which is a short distance from the supposed mines.

"Here they were approached by the third army of the King of Angola, so numerous that it extended for two leagues. The Governor attacked it on the 2nd February, 1583, before it had had time to form on the plain below, and with the assistance of several native chiefs fell on the black multitude with such success as to disperse it completely in a few hours, leaving the field covered with dead. Paulo Diaz ordered the noses of all the slain to be cut off, and sent several loads of them to Loanda as evidence of his victory, and to inspire the blacks with the fear of his arms. The King of Angola, rendered desperate by these repeated defeats, attempted with a fourth army to obtain a victory over the Portuguese, but was again routed with great slaughter. In celebration of the above victory Paulo Diaz founded the first settlement in the interior at Massangano, under the title of Nossa Senhora da Victoria.

"In 1597, 200 Flemish colonists arrived at Loanda, but nearly the whole of them quickly died from the effects of the climate.

"About the same time the colony of Benguella was founded by a party of seventy soldiers, but fifty of these having walked out unarmed on the beach, to amuse themselves by fishing, were surprised by a large number of blacks, who cut their heads off, and then attacked the twenty men in the fort. They defended themselves bravely until all but two, who managed to escape, were killed.

"Constantly engaged in wars with the powerful 'Sobas' and savage populous nations of the interior, the Portuguese gradually extended and established their power in Angola.

"In 1595, Jeronymo d'Almeida, with 400 men and twenty-one horses, again started from Loanda to take possession of the silver mines of Cambambe, and on his way established the fort at Muxima on the River Quanza. Continuing his march, he fell ill, and was obliged to return to Loanda, leaving his officers in command. These were unfortunately drawn into an ambuscade in a rocky ravine at Cambambe, where, an immense number of blacks falling on them, 206 of the Portuguese were slain, notwithstanding their bravest resistance, and only seven men escaped the wholesale slaughter.

"In the same year João Furtado de Mendonça arrived at Loanda, bringing with him twelve white women, the first that had ever arrived in Angola, and who are said to have all married immediately.

"The new Governor's first acts were to retrieve the losses suffered by his predecessor, but starting in the worst season of the year, he remained some time on the banks of the River Bengo, where 200 men died of fever, the rest suffering greatly from hunger. At last, continuing his march with the remains of his force, he very successfully reduced the rebellious 'Sobas' to obedience, and relieving the little garrison at Massangano, inflicted great loss on the blacks in a battle at that place. Returning down the River Quanza, he re-established at Muxima the fort that had been abandoned.

"In 1602, João Rodrigues Coutinho arrived as Governor with reinforcements of men and ammunition, and full powers to promote the conquest of the silver mines of Cambambe. A powerful and well-appointed expedition again started for this purpose, but on arriving at a place called Cacullo Quiaquimone he fell ill and died. Manoel Cerveira Pereira, his successor, resolving to carry out his predecessor's intentions, marched into Cambambe, and on the 10th August, 1603, offered battle to the Soba Cafuxe, whom he defeated in a great engagement; continuing his march he built a fort in Cambambe and forced the Soba Cambambe to submit.

"About 1606, the first attempt was made to communicate across the continent of Africa with the River Senna, on the eastern coast, and for this expedition Balthazar Rebello de Aragão was chosen, but after proceeding for a considerable distance he was obliged to return to relieve the garrison at Cambambe, closely besieged by the blacks.

"Though constant wars were necessary to reduce the warlike Sobas of the interior to obedience, the successes of the Portuguese continued, and their efforts were also directed to the conquest of Benguella and settlement there.

"In the year 1621, the famous Queen Ginga Bandi came to Loanda as head of an embassy from her brother, the Gola Bandi; she arranged a treaty of peace with the Portuguese, was converted to Christianity and baptized under the name of Ginga Donna Anna de Souza. She was proclaimed Queen of Angola on the death of her brother, whom she ordered to be poisoned, never forgiving him for having killed her son. She then not only forsook Christianity, but forgetting the manner in which she had been treated by the Portuguese, bore them a deadly hatred for upwards of thirty years, during which time she was unsuccessful in all her wars against them.

"The Dutch, who for several years had greatly annoyed the Portuguese on the West Coast, attempted to possess themselves of some of their ports for the purpose of obtaining a supply of slaves for their colonies in America. During the governorship of Fernan de Souza the Dutch despatched a fleet of eight ships commanded by Petri Petrid, who attempted to force the bar of Loanda, but meeting with a determined resistance retired from the coast after a stay of three months, having only captured four small vessels.

"The Count of Nassau, considering that without an abundant supply of slaves from the west coast the Dutch possessions in America would be of little value, determined to take stronger measures for obtaining them, and sent a powerful fleet of twenty vessels, under the command of General Tolo. On the 24th August, 1641, this formidable fleet appeared at Loanda, and such was the consternation it caused that the Governor and inhabitants abandoned the city and retired to Bembem. The Dutch landing next day became, without opposition, masters of the place and of a large booty.

"Pedro Cezar retired to the River Bengo, but, pursued by the Dutch, retired to Massangano, where the Portuguese suffered terribly from the effects of the climate. Many of the native chiefs, taking advantage of the occasion, rose in arms against them. Queen Ginga and several other powerful chiefs immediately formed an alliance with the Dutch. The Portuguese attempted, but unsuccessfully, to punish several of them. The Dutch subsequently formed a truce with the Portuguese, in consequence of news arriving from Europe of a treaty of peace having been concluded between the two powers; but shortly after, treacherously attacking the Portuguese, they killed the principal officers and forty men, and took the Governor and 120 men prisoners.

"Those that escaped fled to Massangano until another truce was concluded, and means were found to enable Pedro Cezar to escape from the fortress of San Miguel, where he was imprisoned.

"Francisco de Soutomayor now arrived from Portugal as Governor of Angola, and with the remnant of the troops at Benguella, where he had landed, proceeded to Massangano, without knowledge of the enemy. Queen Ginga, influenced secretly by the Dutch, was collecting her forces for the purpose of attacking the Portuguese, but was completely defeated, leaving 2000 blacks dead on the field of battle. A few days after, the Dutch again broke their truce, and the Portuguese, incensed at their repeated treachery, declared war against them. Thus they remained till the arrival of Salvador Correa de Sá e Benavides, Governor of Rio Janeiro, from which place he started in May, 1648, with a fleet of fifteen vessels and 900 men. Towards the expenses of this expedition the inhabitants of Rio Janeiro largely contributed, as they saw how hurtful to their interests the loss of Angola would be from the failure in the supply of slave labour.

"Arrived at Loanda, he sent a message to the Dutch Governor that although his orders were to preserve peace with him, still, as he had so treacherously and repeatedly broken it with the Portuguese, he considered himself free to declare war against him; but, to prevent bloodshed, he gave the Dutch the option of surrendering, assuring them of an honourable capitulation. The Dutch asked for eight days to consider; Salvador Correa accorded them two, at the end of which he sent his secretary on shore, with orders to signal whether the Dutch accepted his terms or meant to defend themselves; they chose the latter, and the Portuguese immediately landed, and invested the fortress of San Miguel. The Dutch had abandoned six guns, these with four others from the ships were the same night planted on two batteries, and the fortress bombarded. This not having the desired effect, Salvador Correa ordered a general attack. The Portuguese were, however, repulsed with a loss of 163 men killed and wounded. The Dutch, unaware of this great loss, and expecting a second attack, hoisted a white flag, and sent to arrange the terms of capitulation, which being done, the gates, on the 15th of August, 1648, were thrown open, and there issued forth 1100 Dutch, German, and French infantry, and as many blacks, who were all surprised, on passing the Portuguese troops, at the smallness of their numbers, and repented their hasty submission. Salvador Correa sent them all on board three vessels to await their countrymen away in the interior. On their arrival these were also placed on board, and they set sail the same day. Shortly after he caused the Dutch establishments at Pinda and Loango to be demolished, and their expulsion being completed, he next fell on and defeated the native chiefs.

"It was in the time of this Governor that the Italian Capuchin Friars passed from the kingdom of Congo to Loanda, to establish in the interior their excellent missions. For several years the Portuguese waged a constant war with the Libollos, the Quissamas, the Soba N'golla Caboco, the Chiefs of Benguella, and the Dembos Ambuillas at Encoge.

"In the year 1694 the first copper coinage was introduced from Portugal into Angola, the currency up to that time being in the shape of little straw mats called 'Libongos,' of the value of fifty reis each (about 2*d*.). (These little mats are at present only employed as money in Cabinda.)

"In 1758, the Portuguese established themselves at Encoge. In 1783, an expedition was despatched to the Port of Cabinda, to establish a fort; 300 men, however, quickly died there from the effects of the climate, and the rest surrendered to a French squadron, sent to demolish any fortifications that might impede the free commerce of all nations on the coast of Loango.

"Shortly after 1784, the Portuguese had a great war with the natives of Mossulo, which lasted some five years before they were finally defeated.

"It was during the government, and by the efforts of Antonio de Saldanha da Gama (1807-1810), that direct intercourse was established with the nation of the Moluas, and through their intervention overland communication with the eastern coast was obtained.

"The first attempt to communicate directly across the continent, from Angola to Moçambique, was made as already noticed in the year 1606. Two expeditions were proposed to start simultaneously from Moçambique and Angola, and meet in the interior. The former, under the command of the naturalist, Dr. Lacerda, started from the River Senna, and reached Cazembe, where Lacerda fell a victim to the insalubrity of the climate.

"Antonio de Saldanha, anxious to realize a project so interesting to geographical knowledge, and which he judged might besides be of great importance to Portugal, had renewed the inquiries and investigations that might suggest the means of attaining its accomplishment. At Pungo Andongo, there lived one Francisco Honorato da Costa, Lieutenant-Colonel of Militia, a clever man, and Chief of Cassange, the farthest inland of the Portuguese vassal provinces. Through him Antonio de Saldanha learnt that the territory of the Jaga, or Soba of Cassange, was bounded to the east by another and more powerful kingdom, that of the Moluas, with whom the Jaga was in constant intercourse, but whom he prevented from treating directly with the Portuguese, so as to derive the great advantage of monopolizing all the trade with the latter. For this end the Jaga employed several absurd statements to intimidate the Muata Yamba, or King of the Moluas, whose power he feared, telling him that the Portuguese (or white men) issued out of the sea, that they devoured negroes, that the goods he traded in were manufactured in his dominions, and that if the Moluas invaded these, the Portuguese would avenge him.

"As soon as the Governor was informed of these particulars, he ordered Honorato to make himself acquainted with the position of the nation of the Moluas. Honorato succeeded in sending his 'Pombeiros' (black traders) to their principal town, where the Muata Yamba resided, and where they were hospitably received. Convinced by them of the falsehoods of the Jaga Cassange, the Muata, though still in fear, decided to send his wife, who lived at some distance off, on an embassy to the same effect to Loanda.

Accompanied by Honorato's 'Pombeiros,' the embassy, unable to pass the territory of the Soba Cassange, through his opposition, proceeded to the country of the Soba Bomba, who not only allowed them free passage, but likewise sent an ambassador to the Portuguese. They arrived in January, 1808, at Loanda, where they were received in state by the Governor.

"On arriving at the door of the audience-room, they advanced towards the General with great antics, and delivered to him the presents they had brought, which consisted of slaves, a zebra skin, several skins of 'ferocious monkeys,' a mat, some straw baskets, two bars of copper, and a sample of salt from Cazembe. After receiving the greatest hospitality, they were sent back with presents for their respective sovereigns. The ambassadors wore long beards, their heads adorned with a great bunch of parrots' feathers, grey and red, their arms and legs covered with brass and iron rings; from a large monkey skin twisted and hanging from one shoulder depended a large knife,—in their left hand a spear, in the right a horse's tail, as an emblem of authority, and round the waist a striped cloth, over which hung a monkey skin, giving them altogether a very wild and showy appearance. The 'Pombeiros' described the Moluas as a somewhat civilized nation; that the 'Banza,' or town of the Muata, was laid out in streets and shaded in summer, to mitigate the heat of the sun and prevent dust; that they had a flour and grain market for the housing and regular distribution of provisions, and many squares or open spaces of large extent.

"The wife of the Muata lived at a distance from him of thirty or forty leagues, in a country where she reigned as Queen absolute, and only saw her husband on certain days in the year. The executions in the 'Banza' of the Queen amounted to eight, ten, and fifteen blacks per day, and it is probable that in that of the Muata the number was not less. The barbarity of their laws, and the want of communications by means of which to get rid of their criminals, was the cause of this horrible number of executions."

Feo Cardozo, who expresses himself most strongly against slavery, here observes: "Despite the theories and declamation of sensitive minds led away by false notions of the state of the question, as long as the barbarity and ignorance of the African nations shall exist, the barter of slaves will always be considered by enlightened philanthropists as the only palliative to the ferocity of the laws that govern those nations.

"It was further ascertained from the 'Pombeiros,' that the nation of Cazembe, where Dr. Lacerda had died, was feudatory to the Muata Yamba, and in token of its vassalage paid him a yearly tribute of sea salt, obtained from the eastern coast. The possibility of communication with the east coast through the interior being now evident, the Governor Saldanha instructed the 'Pombeiros' to retrace their steps towards the east, and continue in that direction.

"It was during the succeeding Governorship of José d'Oliveira Barboza, however, that the feasibility of such communication was finally proved, for he sought out a black trader to go to Moçambique across the interior, and return by the same route, bringing back answers from the Governor of that Colony to letters sent him from Loanda. This fact added nothing to geographical knowledge, from the ignorance of the man who accomplished it.

"In 1813, this Governor formed the plan of conveying the waters of the River Quanza into the city of Loanda, from a distance of about fourteen leagues, by means of a canal, which was commenced in that year, and the workings continued during 1814 and 1815, but abandoned after being cut for a length of 3000 fathoms, on account of the difficulties encountered for want of a previous survey."

No attempt has since been made to supply the city with water from the Quanza, or from the still nearer River Bengo; besides the great boon such a work would confer on the hot and dry town, it could not fail to be a great success from a monetary point of view.

PLATE I.
TRAVELLING IN ANGOLA—VIEW NEAR AMBRIZ.

CHAPTER II.
PHYSICAL GEOGRAPHY—CHARACTER OF VEGETATION—RIVERS.

The Portuguese possessions of Angola on the south-west coast of Africa extend from Ambriz in 7° 49′ S. Lat. to Cape Frio in 18° 20′ S. Lat. Their farthest establishment south is, however, at Mossamedes, or Little Fish Bay, in 15° 20′ S. Lat.

Throughout this book in speaking of Angola I include not only the country from Mossamedes to Ambriz, at present occupied by the Portuguese, but farther north, as far as the River Congo, that being its strong natural limit of climate, fauna, and ethnology, as I shall further explain.

This long extent of coast comprises, as may be readily imagined, considerable variety in geological formation, physical configuration, climate, vegetation, and natural productions, tribes of natives, and different languages, habits, and customs.

The coast-line is nowhere very bold; level sandy bays, fringed with a belt of the dark evergreen mangrove, alternate with long stretches of cliffs, seldom attaining any great height or grandeur, and covered with a coarse branching grass (*Eragrostis* sp.), small patches of shrubby scrub, a tall cactus-like tree Euphorbia, and the gigantic towering Baobab with its fantastic long gourd-like fruit. (Plate I.)

The "Calema," or surf-wave, with its ceaseless roar, breaks heavily in long white lines on the smooth beach, and pulverizes the hardest rock, and every particle of shell and animal structure. It dashes against the base of the cliffs, resounding loudly in its mad fury as it has done, wave after wave and hour after hour, for unknown ages; and the singular absence of gulls or any moving living objects, or noises, to divert the eye or ear from the dreadful monotony of constantly recurring sound, and line after line of dazzling white foam, gives a distinctive and excessively depressing character to the coast, in harmony, as it were, with the enervating influence of its climate.

The character of the Angolan landscape is entirely different from that of the West Coast proper; say from Cape Verde to the Gaboon and the River Congo. Along that great length of coast are hundreds of square miles of brackish and salt-water lagoons and swamps, level with the sea, and often only separated from it by a narrow mangrove-fringed beach. The bottom of these lagoons is generally a soft deep black fetid mud, and a stick plunged into it comes up thickly covered with a mass nearly approaching in appearance to paste blacking. In the dry season great expanses of the bottom of these swamps become partially dry, and fermenting in the hot tropical sun cause a horrible stench, from the decayed millions of small fish, crabs, &c., left exposed on the surface. The number of fish and some of the lower forms of life inhabiting the mud and water of the lagoons is almost incredible. If one keeps quite still for a few minutes, the slimy ground becomes perfectly alive and hissing from the legions of small brightly coloured land crabs that issue simultaneously from thousands of round holes, from the size of a quill to about an inch and a-half in diameter.

It is in these gigantic hotbeds of decomposition that the deadly types of African fever are, I believe, mostly generated; and these pest waters and mud, when swept into the rivers by the floods in the rainy season, are carried far and wide, with what effect to human life on that coast it is needless to mention.

On those parts of the West Coast where level swampy ground is not the rule, a most agreeable change is seen in the character of the landscape, although, perhaps, the climate is just as unhealthy. Drenched constantly by pelting thunderstorms, and drizzling mists that roll down from the high lands and mountain-tops, the country is covered by the most luxuriant forest vegetation, in one expanse of the deepest unvarying green, the combined result of excessive moisture and the tropical sun of an almost uninterrupted summer.

This alternation of swamp and dense forest ends completely on arriving at the River Congo, and a total change to the comparatively arid country of Angola takes place; in fact, at about 13° S. Lat. it becomes almost a perfectly arid, rocky, and sandy desert.

I may say that, without exception, from the River Congo to Mossamedes no dense forest is seen from the sea, and from thence not a single tree, it is said, for hundreds of miles to the Orange River. A little mangrove, lining the insignificant rivers and low places in their vicinity, is all that varies the open scrub, of which the giant Adansonias and Euphorbias have taken, as it were, exclusive possession. Nowhere on the coast is seen more than an indication of the wonderful vegetation, or varied beauty and fertility, which generally begins at a distance of from thirty to sixty miles inland.

At this distance, a ridge or hilly range runs along the whole length of Angola, forming the first elevation; a second elevation succeeds it at about an equal distance; and a third, at perhaps twice the distance again, lands us on the central high plateau of Africa.

From the few and insignificant streams traversing Angola to the coast, which at most only reach sufficiently far inland to have their source at this third elevation or central plateau, it would seem that a great central depression or fall drains the waters of that part of Africa in either an easterly or southerly direction.

I think it is very doubtful whether the Congo, with its vast body of water and rapid current, drains any large extent of country in an easterly direction to the interior, beyond the first rapids. The gradual elevation from the coast to the ridge beyond which the central plateau begins, and from which the streams that drain Angola seem to have their source, may have been formed by the upheaval of the country by volcanic action. Of this there is evidence in the trachytes and basalts of Cambambe and the country to the south of Benguella, which form an anticlinal axis running the whole length of Angola, and thus prevent the drainage of the interior to the sea on this part of the coast.

These successive elevations inland are accompanied by very remarkable changes in the character of the vegetation covering the surface of the country, and in my several excursions and explorations to the interior from Ambriz to Bembe, from Loanda to the Pungo Andongo range, from Novo Redondo to Mucelis, and to the interior of Benguella and Mossamedes, I have had frequent opportunities of remarking these very singular and sudden changes. These are due, I believe, as Dr. Welwitsch has pointed out, to the difference of elevation alone, irrespective of its geological formation.

A sketch of the vegetation of the country traversed by the road from Ambriz to Bembe, where is situated the wonderful deposit of malachite,—a distance of about 120 miles E.N.E.—will give an idea of the general character of the change observed in travelling towards the interior of Angola. For about twenty-five miles from Ambriz the vegetation is, as already described, principally composed of enormous Baobabs, Euphorbias, a tall Agave (or aloe), a tree called "Muxixe" by the natives, bearing curious seed-pods (*Sterculia tomentosa*), a few small slender creepers, great abundance of the *Sansevieria Angolensis* in the thickets of prickly bushes, and coarse short tufty grasses,—the branching grass being only found near the coast for a few miles. The country is pretty level, dry, and stony, of weathered large-grained gneiss. At Matuta the scene suddenly and magically changes, and in so striking a manner as to impress even the most unobservant traveller. The Baobabs become much fewer in number, the Agaves, the Sansevieria, the Euphorbias, suddenly and almost completely disappear, as also do most of the prickly shrubs, the fine trailing and creeping plants, the Muxixe, and several other trees, and a number of smaller plants. A new set of larger, shadier trees and shrubs take their place, the grass becomes tall and broad-leaved, and one seems to be travelling in an entirely new country.

This character is preserved for another stretch of road till Quiballa is reached, about sixty miles from the coast, where the rise in level is more marked; and again the vegetation changes, almost as remarkably as at Matuta, where, however, the difference in altitude is not so sudden, but a gradual rise is noticed all the way from Ambriz. Creepers of all kinds, attaining a gigantic size, here almost monopolize the vegetation, clasping round the biggest trees, and covering them with a mass of foliage and flower, and forming most exquisite festoons and curtains as they web, as it were, one tree to another in their embrace. No words can describe the luxuriance of these tree creepers, particularly in the vicinity of the shallow rivers and rivulets of the interior. Several trees together, covered from top to bottom with a rich mantle of the India-rubber creeper (*Landolphia florida?*), with bright, large dark-green leaves somewhat resembling those of the magnolia, thickly studded with large bunches of purest white jasmine-like flowers, loading the air for a considerable distance with its powerful bitter-almond perfume, and attracting a cloud of buzzing insects, form altogether a sight not easily forgotten. Once at Bembe I saw a perfect wall or curtain formed by a most delicate creeper, hung from top to bottom with bottle-brush-like flowers about three inches long;—but the grandest view presented to my eyes was in the Pungo Andongo range, where the bottom of a narrow valley, for quite half a mile in length, was filled, as they all are in the interior, by a dense forest of high trees; the creepers, in search of light, had pierced through and spread on the top, where their stems and leaves had become woven and matted into a thick carpet on which their flowers were produced in such profusion that hardly a leaf was visible, but only one long sea of beautiful purple, like a glacier of colour—filling the valley and set in the frame of green of the luxuriant grass-covered hill sides. The very blacks that accompanied me, so little impressed as they are usually by the beauties of nature, beat their open mouths with the palm of the hand as they uttered short "Ah! ah! ahs!" their universal mode of expressing astonishment or delight, so wonderful, even to them, appeared the magnificent mass of colour below us as it suddenly came in view when we arrived at the head of the valley, down one side of which we descended to the plain below.

I have seen the surface of a large pool of water thickly covered with a layer of purple pea-shaped flowers, fallen from the large Wistaria-like bunches of blossom of a creeper overgrowing a mass of trees standing at the edge: it seemed as if Nature, loth that so much beauty should fade quickly, had kept for some time longer the fallen flowers fresh and lovely on the cool still water of the shady lake. This abundance of creeping plants is more or less preserved till at about sixty miles farther inland we arrive at Bembe and the comparatively level country stretching away to the interior; the oil-palm (*Elæis Guineensis*) then becomes again abundant, these trees being only found on the coast in any number in the vicinity of the rivers; the beautiful feathery papyrus also again covers the lagoons and wet places.

The comparatively short and spare thin-leaved and delicate tufted grasses of the first or littoral region are succeeded in the second, as I have already said, by much stronger kinds, attaining an extraordinary development in the highest or third region. Gigantic grasses from five to as much as sixteen feet high, growing luxuriantly, cover densely the vast plains and tracts of country in these two regions where tree vegetation is scarce. The edges of the blades of most of these tall grasses are so stiff and finely and strongly serrated as to be quite sharp, and if passed quickly over the skin will cause a deep cut, as clean as if done with a knife; one species is called by the natives "Capim de faca" in Portuguese, or "knife grass," from the manner in which it cuts if handled, or in going through it.

I have often had my hands bleeding from cuts inflicted by this grass when in going down steep, dry, slippery places I have clutched at the high grass on each side of me to prevent falling. To any one accustomed to grass only a few inches high, the dimensions that these species attain are simply incredible. Like snow and ice in northern latitudes, grasses in interior tropical Africa for some six months in the year take undisputed possession of the country and actually interrupt all communication in many places.

It is a very strange feeling when travelling in a hammock, to be forced through grass so dense and so high that nothing but the sky above can be seen,—a wall of dry rustling leaves on each side shutting out all view sometimes for mile after mile, and so intensely hot and breathless as to be almost unbearable, causing the perspiration to run in drops off the wet, shining, varnished skins of the almost naked blacks. In going through places where the grass has nearly choked up all signs of a path, it is necessary to send in advance all the blacks of the party, so as to open aside and widen it sufficiently to allow the traveller in his hammock to be carried and pushed through the dense high mass: even if there be a moderate breeze blowing it is, of course, completely shut out; the perspiration from the negroes is wiped on the grass as they push through it, now shoving it aside with their hands and arms, now forcing their way through it backwards, and it is most disagreeable to have the wetted leaves constantly slapping one's face and hands, to say nothing of the horrible stink from their steaming bodies. It is a powerful odour, and the quiet hot air becomes so impregnated with it as to be nearly overpowering. It is difficult to compare it with any other disagreeable animal smell; it is different from that of the white race, and the nearest comparison I can give is a mixture of putrid onions and rancid butter well rubbed on an old billy-goat. In some it is a great deal worse than in others, but none, men or women, are free from it, even when their bodies are at rest or not sensibly perspiring; and it being a natural secretion of the skin, of course no amount of washing or cleanliness will remove it. The mulattoes, again, have it, but different, and not generally so strong as the pure black, and with a more acid odour, reminding one strongly of the caprylic and similar acids known to chemists. The natives themselves naturally do not notice it, and after some time of residence in the country, except in very powerful cases, strangers become comparatively accustomed to it, and, as showing how a person may in time become used to nastiness, I have even partaken of a dish in which were some forcemeat balls that I had previously watched the negro cook roll with the palm of his hand on his naked stomach, to make them of a proper round shape, without spoiling my appetite or preventing me from joining in the deserved praise of the stew that contained them.

The Portuguese and Brazilians call the smell that exhales from the bodies of the blacks "Catinga," and I witnessed an amusing instance of its effect on a dog, when it smelt it for the first time. On my second voyage to Angola, I took with me a beautiful "perdigueiro," or Portuguese pointer, from Lisbon; this animal had evidently never smelt a negro before our arrival at Ilha do Principe (Prince's Island); for, on two of the blacks from the custom-house boat coming on the poop, it began sniffing the air at some distance from where they were standing, and carefully and slowly approached them with its neck and nose at full stretch, with a look on its intelligent face of the greatest curiosity and surprise. On approaching within three or four yards, the smell of the blacks, who kept quite still, being afraid it might bite them, seemed too much for its sensitive nose, and it sneezed and looked perfectly disgusted. It continued to approach them and sneeze and retreat repeatedly for some little time, evidently unable to get used to the powerful perfume. The poor dog's unmistakeable expression of thorough dislike to the odour of the black race was most comical.

An old Brazilian mule that I had at Benguella could not bear the blacks to saddle her or put her bridle and head-gear on; she would throw back her ears, and suddenly make a snap with her teeth at the black who attempted it. She was a very tame animal, and would be perfectly quiet to a white man. She had been seventeen years in Benguella before she came into my possession, but never became used to negroes; whether she disliked them from their disagreeable odour, or from some other reason, I could not discover; but, judging from the dog's decided antipathy, I presume their smell was her principal objection, and yet it is very singular that wild animals in Africa will scent a white sooner than a black hunter. I have heard this from many persons in Angola, both blacks and whites. It would be interesting to know if our hunters at the Cape have noticed the same thing. The fact that, notwithstanding the "Catinga," black hunters can lie in ambush, and antelope and other game come so close to them that they can fire the whole charge of their flint muskets, wadding and all, into them, is well known in Angola.

Whilst exploring for minerals in Cambambe, I was prevented for a long time from visiting several localities, from the paths to them being choked up with grass. It is difficult to imagine how exhausting it is to push through thick, high grass; in a very short time one becomes completely out of breath, and the arms hang powerless with the exertion: the heat and suffocating stillness of the air may have as much to do with this as the amount of force exerted to push aside the yielding, rustling mass.

Shortly after the rains cease in May, the grass, having flowered and attained its full growth, rapidly dries up under the hot sun, and is then set on fire by the blacks, forming the wonderful "Queimadas," literally "burnings," of the Portuguese, and "smokes" of the English in the Bights. If only the leaves are sufficiently dry to catch fire, the stems are left green, with a black ring at every joint or base of the leaf, and the mass of whip-like stems then looks like a forest of long porcupine quills. This is very disagreeable to travel through, as the half-burnt stems spring back and cross in every direction behind the front bearer of the hammock, and poke into the traveller's face, and thrash the hands when held up to save the eyes from injury, and after a day's journey one gets quite black, with eyes and throat sore and parched from the charcoal dust and fine alkaline ash.

When the grass has become thoroughly dry, the effect of the "Queimada" is indescribably grand and striking. In the daytime the line of fire is marked by a long cloud of beautiful white steam-like smoke curling slowly up, dense and high in the breathless air, in the most fantastic forms against the clear blue sky. This cloud of smoke is closely accompanied by a perfect flock of rapacious birds of every size and description, from the magnificent eagle to the smallest hawk, circling and sailing high and grandly in the air, and now and then swooping down upon the unfortunate rats, mice, and small animals, snakes, and other reptiles, burnt and left exposed by the conflagration. Near the blazing grass the scene is very fine, a deafening noise is heard as of thousands of pistol shots, caused by the imprisoned air bursting every joint of the long stems, and the loud rush and crackling of the high sheet of flame, as it catches and consumes the dry upright straw. One is inspired with awe and a feeling of puny insignificance before the irresistible march of the flames that are rapidly destroying the enormous extent of the dense, nearly impenetrable mass of vegetation covering the surface of the country, leaving it perfectly bare with the exception of a few charred root stumps of grass, and a few stunted, scorched shrubs and trees. At night the effect is wonderfully fine: the vast wall of fire is seen over hill and valley, as far as the eye can reach; above the brilliant leaping flames, so bright in the clear atmosphere of the tropical night, vast bodies of red sparks are shot up high into the cloud of smoke, which is of the most magnificent lurid hue from the reflection of the grand blaze below.

No trees or shrubs are consumed by the burning of the grasses, everything of a larger growth being too green to take fire; a whitening or drying of the leaves is generally the only effect even where the light annual creepers growing on them have been consumed. Forest or jungle in Angola, unlike other countries, never burns, and is consequently the refuge of all the larger animals and birds from the "Queimadas," which are undoubtedly the cause in many parts of Angola of the great scarcity of animal and insect life which strikes a traveller expecting to meet everywhere the great abundance known to exist in the interior.

Great is the alarm of the natives on the near approach of these fires to their towns, the whole population turning out, and with branches of trees beating out the fire. It is seldom, however, that their huts are consumed, as the villages are generally situated in places where trees and shrubs abound, and the different huts are mostly separated by hedges of different species of Euphorbiaceæ. Many villages are entirely surrounded by a thick belt of these milky-juiced plants, effectually guarding them from any chance of fire from the grass outside. Where the huts are not thus protected, the danger, of course, is very great, but the natives sometimes take the precaution of setting fire to patches of the grass to clear a space around the huts or village. There is no danger in travelling from these grass fires, for, when they are seen approaching, their rate of progress being slow, it is sufficient to set fire to the dry grass to leeward to clear a space in which to encamp in safety.

The change in vegetation is also accompanied by difference of climate, but it is difficult to say whether they react on each other, and if so, in what proportion. The rains are very much more abundant and constant towards the interior of the country, where the vegetation is densest: on the coast the rains are generally very deficient, and some seasons entirely fail; this is more especially the case south of about 12° Lat., several successive rainy seasons passing without a single drop of rain falling. A three years' drought in the interior of Loanda is still vividly remembered, the inhabitants, from their improvident habits, perishing miserably by thousands from starvation. In my mining explorations at Benguella, I was at Cuio under a cloudless sky for twenty-six months, in the years 1863 and 1864, with hardly a drop of water falling.

I had under my charge at that time twenty-four white men, and between 400 and 600 blacks at work on a copper deposit, mining and carrying ore to the coast, distant about four miles; and no one accustomed to a constant supply of water, can imagine the anxiety and work I had to go through to obtain the necessary amount for that large number of thirsty people, very often barely sufficient for drinking purposes; no water fit for drinking or cooking was to be had nearer than six miles, and as no bullock carts could be employed, it had all to be carried in kegs on men's shoulders, and by a troop of the most miserable, small, idiotically stubborn donkeys that can be imagined from the Cape de Verde Islands. It was impossible always to be looking after the blacks told off daily on water duty, and words cannot express the annoyance and vexation that the rascals constantly caused us, by getting drunk on the road, wilfully damaging the kegs, selling the water to natives on their way back, bringing the filthiest water out of muddy pools instead of clear from the proper place, sleeping on the road, and keeping all waiting, sometimes without a drop of water, very often till far into the night. This was no joke when we were thirsty, hungry, dusty, and tired, after a hot day's work blasting rock, breaking up copper ore in the sun at the mine in the bottom of a circular valley, where the little air above seldom reached, and where the dazzling white sand and gneiss rock, bare of nearly all vegetation, reflected and intensified the glare and heat almost unbearably in the hot season.

In going from north to south the character of the vegetation changes very insensibly from the River Congo to Mossamedes. As far as Ambrizzette the Mateba palm (*Hyphæne Guineensis*) is very abundant. This palm-tree, unlike the oil-palm, which is only found near water, or in rich soil, grows on the dry cliffs and country of the littoral region very abundantly as far as about Ambriz. The leaves of this palm-tree are employed to make small bags, in which most of the ground-nuts are exported from the coast. The Cashew-tree (*Anacardium occidentale*) grows on this part of the coast from Congo to Ambrizzette still more abundantly, in many places there being hardly any other tree or shrub; it is also very plentiful again around Loanda, but to the south it nearly disappears. A thin stemmy Euphorbia, nearly leafless, is a principal feature of the landscape about Loanda, and gives it a very dull and arid appearance. The cactus-like, upright Euphorbia is a notable characteristic of the whole coast of Angola.

South of Benguella the country is extremely arid, the gneiss, gypsum, and basalt, of which it is principally composed, appearing only to afford nourishment to a very limited vegetation, both in number or species, principally spiny trees and shrubs with numbers of dreadful recurved prickles, nearly bare of leaves a great part of the year,—and over immense tracts of very uneven ground even these are scarce: only the gigantic Euphorbias, and the stunted roots of grass sparingly distributed, break the monotony of a silent, dry, rocky desert.

A very curious creeper, a species of Cassytha, is extremely abundant in Benguella, covering the shrubs and small trees closely with its network of leafless string-like stems. The *Sansevieria Angolensis* is very plentiful all over the littoral region of Angola; the flat-leaved species (*S. longiflora*) is only noticed north from Ambriz to Congo, and only growing very near the sea: the S. Angolensis is but rarely seen with it, and it is very curious how distinctly these two species are separated. In the immediate vicinity of all the rivers and streams of Angola the vegetation is, as might be expected, generally very luxuriant, particularly north of Benguella.

The total absence of horned cattle among the natives on the coast, from the River Congo to south of the River Quanza, is very remarkable; due, I believe, as much to some influence of climate, or poisonous or irritant nature of the vegetation, as to the neglect of the natives to breed them, though a few small herds of cattle to be seen at Ambrizzette and Quissembo belonging to the white traders, and brought by the natives far from the interior, appear to thrive very well, and several Portuguese have bred fine herds at the River Loge, about three miles from Ambriz; they would not thrive, however, at Bembe, where those that were purchased from the ivory caravans from the interior gradually became thin and died. The natives south of the Quanza beyond the Quissama country, as far as Mossamedes, breed large numbers of cattle—their principal wealth, in fact, consisting of their herds. The district of Loanda cannot supply itself with cattle sufficient for its moderate consumption, a large proportion having to be brought from Cambambe and Pungo Andongo and even much farther from the interior.

South of the Congo there is only one navigable river, the Quanza, in 9° 20′ S., and even the bar and mouth of this are shifty, and so shallow as only to admit vessels drawing not more than five or six feet of water, and this only at high tides. The Rivers Dande and Bengo are only navigable by barges for a few miles; others, such as the Ambrizzette, Loge, Novo Redondo, Quicombo, Egito, Anha, Catumbella, and Luache, barely admit the entrance of a canoe, and their bars are often closed for a considerable time in the dry season; the beds of others are completely dried up for miles inland at that time of the year, and it is very curious to see the level sandy bed without water between the luxuriant and creeper-covered banks, and the borders of sedge and grass.

Although dry on the surface, cool delicious water is met with at a few inches below. I shall never forget, on my first journey into Cambambe, the haste with which we pushed forward, on an intensely hot morning, in order to arrive at the River Mucozo, a small stream running into the Quanza. We had encamped the night before at a place where only a small supply of water was to be had from a filthy and muddy hole, and so thick and ochrey was it that, even after boiling and straining, it was nearly undrinkable; on reaching the high banks of the Mucozo, great was my disappointment to see the bed of the river one long expanse of dry sand shining in the hot sun, and my hope of water, as I thought, gone! Not so the blacks, who raised a loud shout as they caught sight of it, dashed in a race down the banks, and throwing themselves on the sand quickly scooped out a hole about six inches deep with their hands, and lying flat on their bellies stuck their faces in it, and seemed never to finish drinking to their hearts' content the inexpressibly refreshing, cool, filtered water. After having only dirty and thick water to drink, not improved by coffee or bad rum, after a long, hot day's journey, tired and exhausted, the ground for a bed, mosquitoes, and a smoky fire on each side to keep them off, fleas and other biting things from the sand, that nip and sting but are not seen or caught, snatches of sleep, feverish awakening in the morning, with parched mouth, the perspiration dried on the face and skin, gritty and crystallized and salt to the feel and taste, no water to drink or wash with, the sun out and shining strong again almost as soon as it is daylight, and hurry, hurry, through dry grass and sand without a breath of air, and with the thermometer at 90° in the shade, for four or five hours before we reached the Mucozo—it was no wonder I was disinclined to move from the place till the afternoon came, and the great heat of the day was passed; or that I thought the water, fresh and cold from its clean sandy bed, the most delicious drink that could be imagined!

The delight of a drink of pure cold water in hot climates has over and over again been described by all travellers, but it is impossible to realize it fully without experiencing the sensations that precede and cause the thirst that only cold water seems to satisfy.

The River Luache, at Dombe Grande, near the sea, in the province of Benguella, is dry for some miles inland every year, and its bed of pure, clean, deep sand is as much as half a mile broad at that place. The first great rains in the interior generally come down the dry beds of these rivers suddenly, like a great torrent or wave, and I was fortunate enough to be at Dombe Grande once when the water came down the Luache from the interior. It was a grand sight to see a wave the whole breadth of the river, and I should judge about eight feet high, driving before and carrying with it an immense mass of trees and branches, roots, sedges, and grasses all confused and rolling irresistibly to the sea, with a dull rushing roar, quite unlike the noise one would imagine a body of water to make, but more like a rush of rocks down a mountain in the distance; and very strange and agreeable was the change in the landscape—a broad desert of white sand suddenly transformed into a vast running river of fresh water, bringing gladness to all living things.

The sandy bars of some of the other small rivers of Angola become closed sometimes for several months, but the stream remains of about the same volume, or opens out into a pool or lake, or partly dries up into lovely sedgy pools inhabited by wild-fowl of various kinds, and fields of beautiful aquatic grasses and papyrus plants, in which I have often seen caught by hand the singular fresh-water fish "Bagre" (*Clarias Capensis, Bagrus*, &c.) vigorously alive, left behind by the diminishing waters, in grassy swampy places where the foot hardly sank ankle deep in water, and where it was certainly not deep enough to cover them. The dry sandy beds of rivers in the rainless season are often completely covered with a magnificent growth of the Palma Christi, or Castor Oil plant, with its beautiful large leaves. This I have noticed more particularly in the district of Novo Redondo and Benguella.

Sharks, so frightfully dangerous in the surf of the West Coast, are unknown south of the River Congo. I have never heard of a person being attacked by one, although at Loanda the white population bathe off the island in front of the town, and blacks dabble about in the sea everywhere, and swim to and from the boats and barges.

No strikingly high mountain, I believe, exists in Angola; no hills of any great importance till we arrive at the first rise, which, as we have seen, extends the whole length of Angola at a distance of from thirty to sixty miles from the sea. The second and third elevations contain some fine mountain or hill ranges, as at Bembe, Pungo Andongo, Cazengo, Mucellis, and Capangombe. To the south of Benguella as far as Mossamedes flat-topped or table hills, perfectly bare of vegetation, are a very prominent feature, seen from the sea; they are of basalt, and are about 200 or 300 feet in height, and are in many places the only remains left of a higher level. In others, this higher level still exists for a considerable extent, deeply cut by narrow gorges and ravines leading towards the sea, with nearly perpendicular sides.

CHAPTER III.
THE RIVER CONGO A BOUNDARY—SLAVE TRADE—SLAVERY—ORDEAL BY POISON—INSENSIBILITY OF THE NEGRO—INGRATITUDE.

The River Congo, or Zaire, is a very striking and well-marked line of division or boundary, in respect of climate, fauna, natives and customs, between Angola and the rest of the West Coast.

The difference in the scenery and vegetation from those of the north is very great indeed, and not less so is that of the birds and animals. I have noticed enough to convince me that it would well repay a naturalist to investigate the number of species this river cuts off, as it were, from Angola; the gorilla and chimpanzee, for instance, are only known north of the Congo; they are found at Loango and Landana, and from reports of the natives, even near to the river itself; many species of monkeys, very abundant at Cabinda and on the north bank, are quite unknown in Angola; and the ordinary grey parrot, which is to be seen in flocks on the Congo, is also unknown to the south—the only exception to this rule, as far as I have been able to ascertain, being at Cassange, about 300 miles to the interior of Loanda, where the rare "King parrot," with red feathers irregularly distributed among the grey ones, is not uncommon. Of small birds I have noticed many at Cabinda that I never observed in Angola; the same with butterflies, and other insects.

The Congo is very deep, and the current is always very strong; even above Boma (or M'Boma), about ninety miles distant from the sea, the river is a vast body of water and the current still very swift. From the mouth to beyond this place the banks are deeply cut into innumerable creeks and rivers, and form many large islands. The enormous quantity of fresh water poured by this river into the sea gives rise to many curious speculations as to its extent and probable sources. I am inclined to believe that the River Congo, or its principal branch, after going in a north-east direction for a comparatively short distance, bends to the southward, and will be found to run for many degrees in that direction.

In the preceding chapter we have seen that south of the Congo no river deserving of that name, or draining more than the country up to the third elevation, exists in Angola. The vast country from the River Congo to perhaps the Orange River, or about 1200 miles, has therefore no outfall for its waters into the Atlantic Ocean.

The existence of volcanic rocks in Cambambe and Mossamedes appears to explain the elevation of this part of the coast; how much farther to the south this elevation has taken place is as yet unknown, and I can only reconcile the vast body of water of the River Congo with the absence of any large river farther south, by supposing it to bend down and drain the long line of country upheaved on the seaboard: it is not likely to drain much country to the north from the existence of several rivers such as the Chiloango, Quillo, Massabi, and Mayumba, in a distance of about 360 miles from its mouth to that of the River Gaboon under the Equator.

For many years, and up to about the year 1868, the Congo was the principal shipping place for slaves on the South-West Coast, the large number of creeks in it affording safe hiding-places for loading the ships engaged in the traffic, and the swift current enabling them to go out quickly a long way to sea, and clear the line of cruisers. Boma was the centre or point for the caravans of slaves coming from different parts of the interior, and there was little or no trade in produce.

It may not be out of place here to say a few words on the slave-trade of the South Coast, because a great deal of ignorance and misconception exists on the subject from judging of it as having been similar to the slave-trade in North and East Africa. Repugnant and wicked as is the idea of slavery and dealing in human flesh, philanthropy must be debited with an amount of unknowing cruelty and wholesale sacrifice of life perfectly awful to contemplate, as a set-off against its well-intentioned and successful efforts to put a stop to slavery and the known horrors of the middle passage, and subsequent ill-treatment at the hands of the planters.

In no part of Angola or among tribes to the interior have slave-hunts ever existed as in the north; there are no powerful or more civilized nations making war on weaker tribes for the purpose of obtaining slaves, and devastating the country by fire and sword. There is very little cruelty attending the state of slavery among the natives of Angola, I believe I may say even in the greater part of the rest of tropical Africa, but I will restrict myself to the part of which I have an intimate knowledge. It is a domestic institution, and has existed, as at present, since time immemorial; and there is no more disgrace or discredit in having been born of slave parents, and consequently in being a slave, than there is in Europe in being born of dependents or servants of an ancestral house, and continuing in its service in the same manner.

There is something patriarchal in the state of bondage among the negroes, if we look at it from an African point of view (I must again impress on my readers that all my remarks apply to Angola). The free man, or owner, and his wife, have to supply their slaves with proper food and clothing; to tend them in sickness as their own children, to get them husbands or wives, as the case may be, to supply them with the means of celebrating their festivals, such as their marriages, births, or burials, in nearly the same way as amongst themselves; the slaves, in fact, are considered as their family, and are always spoken of as "my son," or "my daughter." If the daughters of slaves are chosen as wives or concubines by their owners or other free men, it is considered an honour, and their children, though looked upon as slaves, are entitled to special consideration.

There is consequently no cruelty or hardship attending the state of slavery; a male slave cannot be made by his master to cultivate the ground, which is women's work, and the mistress and her slaves till the ground together.

A stranger set down in Angola, and not aware of the existence of slavery, would hardly discover that such an institution prevailed so universally amongst them, so little apparent difference is there between the master and slave. A not very dissimilar condition of things existed in the feudal times in England and other countries. Yet many hundred thousand slaves were brought down to the coast to be sold to the white men and shipped off, and I will now explain how this was the case, paradoxical though it may appear after what I have just said. The number was partly made up of surplus slave population sold off by the owners, probably from inability to feed or clothe them; cases of famine from failure of the crops, from drought, &c., a common local occurrence, also supplied large numbers of slaves; but by far the greatest part were furnished by the effect of their own laws, almost every offence being punishable by slavery, to which not only the guilty party, but even in many cases every member of his family was liable.

Offences against property are especially visited by the severe penalties of slavery, fine, or death. Any one caught in the act of stealing, be the amount ever so small, becomes at once the property or slave of the person robbed. It is a common thing to see blacks working in chains at factories and houses where they have been caught stealing, the custom among the Europeans generally being to detain them until their relatives shall have paid a ransom for them. I must do the natives the justice to say that they are very observant of their own laws, even to a white man alone in their territory, who claims their protection against offenders. Certain offences that we should consider trifling, are by some tribes visited with heavy punishment, such as stealing Indian corn whilst growing, or an egg from under a sitting hen. In other tribes breaking a plate or other article of crockery is a great offence: this is especially the case to the interior of Novo Redondo, where the punishment is death or slavery.

I was told there of the amusing manner in which a Portuguese trader turned the tables on a Soba, or chief of a town, where he had established himself, and who annoyed him greatly by his constant demands for presents, by placing a cracked plate under a sheet on his bed, on which the Soba was in the habit of sitting during his too frequent visits. On the Soba sitting down as usual, on the trap prepared for him, he, of course, smashed the plate to atoms, to his great surprise; frightened at the possible result of the accident, he humbly begged the trader not to let a soul in the place know of it, promising restitution; the wished-for result of the scheme was attained, as he ceased all his importunities during the remainder of the trader's stay in the country.

But all these sources of slaves for shipment were but a fraction of the number supplied by their belief in witchcraft. Witchcraft is their principal, or only belief; every thing that happens has been brought about by it; all cases of drought, sickness, death, blight, accident, and even the most trivial circumstances are ascribed to the evil influence of witchery or "fetish."

A "fetish" man is consulted, and some poor unfortunate accused and either killed at once or sold into slavery, and, in most cases, all his family as well, and every scrap of their property confiscated and divided amongst the whole town; in other cases, however, a heavy fine is imposed, and inability to pay it also entails slavery; the option of trial by ordeal is sometimes afforded the accused, who often eagerly demand it, such is their firm belief in it.

This extremely curious and interesting ordeal is by poison, which is prepared from the thick, hard bark of a large tree, the *Erythrophlæum Guineense* (Oliver, 'Flora of Tropical Africa,' ii. 320). Dr. Brunton has examined the properties of this bark, and finds that it possesses a very remarkable action. The powder, when inhaled, causes violent sneezing; the aqueous extract, when injected under the skin of animals, causes vomiting, and has a remarkable effect upon the vagus nerve, which it first irritates and then paralyses. The irritation of this nerve makes the heart beat slowly. (Fuller details may be found in the 'Proceedings of the Royal Society' for this year.) It is called "casca" by the natives, and I obtained a specimen at Bembe, which was brought to me concealed in rags, by a half-witted water-carrier in my service, and he procured it for me only after my promising him that I would not tell anyone. He said it was from a tree growing about half a day's journey off, but I could not get him to take me to it. The other blacks denied all knowledge of it, and said it was "fetish" for anyone to have it in his possession. On two occasions afterwards, I obtained some more specimens from natives of Cabinda, where the tree is said to be abundant, and the natives very fond of referring all their disputes and accusations to its decision.

"Casca" is prepared by the bark being ground on a stone to a fine powder, and mixed with about half a pint of cold water, a piece about two inches square being said to be a dose. It either acts as an emetic or as a purgative; should the former effect take place, the accused is declared innocent, if the latter, he is at once considered guilty, and either allowed to die of the poison, which is said to be quick in its action, or immediately attacked with sticks and clubs, his head cut off and his body burnt.

All the natives I inquired of agreed in their description of the effect produced on a person poisoned by this bark; his limbs are first affected and he loses all power over them, falls to the ground, and dies quickly; without much apparent suffering.

It is said to be in the power of the "fetish" man to prepare the "casca" mixture in such a manner as to determine which of the effects mentioned shall be produced; in case of a dispute, both parties drink it, and according as he allows the mixture to settle, and gives one the clear liquid and the other the dregs, so does it produce vomiting in the former, and acts as a purgative in the latter case. I have very little doubt that as the "fetish" man is bribed or not, so he can and does prepare it.

The Portuguese in Angola strictly prohibit the use of "casca," and severely punish any natives concerned in a trial by this bark, but it is nevertheless practised in secret everywhere.

The occasion of the test is one of great excitement, and is accompanied by much cruelty. In some tribes the accused, after drinking the potion, has to stoop and pass under half-a-dozen low arches made by bending switches and sticking both ends into the ground; should he fall down in passing under any of the arches, that circumstance alone is sufficient to prove him guilty, without waiting for the purgative effect to be produced.

Before the trial the accused is confined in a hut, closely guarded, and the night before it is surrounded by all the women and children of the neighbouring towns, dancing and singing to the horrid din of their drums and rattles. On the occasion of the ordeal the men are all armed with knives, matchets, and sticks, and the moment the poor devil stumbles in going under one of the switches, he is instantly set upon by the howling multitude and beaten to death, and cut and hacked to pieces in a few minutes. I was at Mangue Grande on one occasion when a big dance was going on the night before a poor wretch was to take "casca." I went to the town with some of the traders at that place, and we offered to ransom him, but to no purpose; nothing, they said, could save him from the trial. I learnt, however, that he passed it successfully, but I think I never heard such a hideous yelling as the 400 or 500 women and children were making round the hut, almost all with their faces and bodies painted red and white, dancing in a perfect cloud of dust, and the whole scene illuminated by blazing fires of dry grass under a starlit summer sky.

The most insignificant and extraordinary circumstances are made the subject of accusations of witchcraft, and entail the usual penalties.

I was at Ambrizzette when three Cabinda women had been to the river with their pots for water; all three were filling them from the stream together, when the middle one was snapped up by an alligator, and instantly carried away under the surface of the water, and of course devoured. The relatives of the poor woman at once accused the other two of bewitching her, and causing the alligator to take her out of their midst! When I remonstrated with them, and attempted to show them the utter absurdity of the charge, their answer was, "Why did not the alligator take one of the end ones then, and not the one in the middle?" and out of this idea it was impossible to move them, and the poor women were both to take "casca." I never heard the result, but most likely one or both were either killed or passed into slavery.

At a place near the mountain range of Pungo Andongo, about 150 miles inland of Loanda, I was once the amused spectator at a curious trial of a man for bewitching the spirit of his dead wife. Her sister, it appeared, suffered from violent headaches, and sleepless nights, which were said to be caused by the wife's spirit being unable to rest, on account of the widower being a wizard. A large circle of spectators was formed round the sick sister, who was squatting on the ground; a fetish man was beating a drum, and singing, or rather droning, some incantation; after a little while, the woman began to give short yelps, and to close her eyes, and on being interrogated by the fetish man, said the spirit of her sister had spoken to her, and that she could not rest until her husband had made restitution of her two goats and her baskets, &c., which he had appropriated, and which she had desired should be given to her sister. The man instantly rose, and brought the goats, baskets, clothes, &c., and laid them before his sister-in-law, and the trial was over. If he had denied the accusation, he would inevitably have had to take "casca."

When we consider the great population of the vast country that supplied the slave trade of the coast, and that, as I have explained, the state of their laws and customs renders all transgressions liable to slavery, the absence of necessity for the slave wars and hunts of the north of Africa and other extensive and thinly populated districts is sufficiently proved. I have been unable to collect positive information as to the statistics of the slaves shipped in Angola (from Congo to Benguella inclusively), but the number could not have been far short of 100,000 per annum. I was told by some of the old inhabitants, that to see as many as ten to twelve vessels loading at a time at Loanda and Benguella was a common occurrence. At the time of the last shipments from Benguella, about ten years ago, I have seen as many as 1000 slaves arrive in one caravan from the interior, principally from Bihé.

Up to within a very few years there existed a marble arm-chair on the wharf at the custom-house at Loanda, where the bishop, in the slave-trading times, was wont to sit, to baptize and bless the batches of poor wretches as they were sent off in barge-loads to the vessels in the harbour. The great slaughter now going on in a great part of Africa, which I have mentioned as the result of the suppression of the slave shipments from the coast, can now be understood; whereas formerly they were sent to the coast to be sold to the white men and exported, they are now simply murdered. On the road down from Bembe in April last, we passed the ashes and bones of a black who had stolen a trade-knife, a bit of iron in a small wooden handle, and made in Germany at the rate of a few shillings per gross, and passed on the coast in trade; on the top of his staff was stuck his skull and the knife he had stolen, a ghastly and lasting warning to passersby of the strict laws of the country respecting property.

If a famine overtakes any part of the country, a common occurrence, the slaves are simply taken out and knocked on the head to save them from starvation. I was told by the natives that the slaves offered no resistance to that fate, but accepted it as inevitable, and preferable to the pangs of hunger, knowing that it was no use going to the coast to save their lives at the hands of the white men by being shipped as slaves. At Musserra, three Cabinda blacks from the boats' crews joined three natives in robbing one of the factories: on complaint being made to the king and principal men of the town, they marched off the three Cabindas, promising to punish them, which they did by cutting off their heads, unknown to the white men; they then brought the three natives to deliver up to the traders as their slaves, but on these refusing to accept them, and demanding that a severe punishment should also be passed on them, they quietly tied a large stone to their necks, took them out in a canoe to the bay, and dropped them into the sea.

It is impossible to reclaim the hordes of savages inhabiting the interior even of Angola from their horrid customs and their disregard for life; the insalubrity of the country, though it is infinitely superior in this respect to the rest of the West Coast, would be an almost insuperable bar to their improvement; their own progress is still more hopeless. In my opinion, it would be necessary that tropical Africa should undergo a total physical revolution, that the long line of unhealthy coast should be upheaved, and the deadly leagues of pestiferous swamps be thus drained, before the country would be fitted for the existence of a higher type of mankind than the present negro race.

It can only have been by countless ages of battling with malaria, that they have been reduced physically and morally to their present wonderful state or condition of withstanding successfully the climatic influences, so fatal to the white and more highly organized race—the sun and fevers of their malignant and dismal mangrove swamps, or the mists and agues of their magnificent tropical forests, no more affecting them than they do the alligators and countless mosquitoes that swarm in the former, or the monkeys and snakes that inhabit the latter. It is really astonishing to see the naked negro, without a particle of covering on his head (often shaved), in the full blaze of the fierce sun, his daily food a few handfuls of ground-nuts, beans, or mandioca-root, and very often most unwholesome water for drink. At night he throws himself on the ground, anywhere, covers himself with a thin grass or cotton cloth, nearly transparent in texture, without a pillow, like a dog, and awakes in the morning generally wet through with the heavy dew, and does not suffer the least pain or inconvenience from the climate from infancy to old age unless his lungs become affected.

The way babies are treated would be enough to kill a white child. The women when at work on the plantations generally place them on a heap of grass or on the ground, and are not at all particular to put them in the shade, and I have often seen them naked and filthy, and covered with a thick mass of large buzzing flies over their faces and bodies, fast asleep, with the sun shining full on them. The women, in carrying them tied behind their backs, seldom include their little heads in the cloth that secures them, but leave them to swing and loll about helplessly in every direction with the movement of walking.

Children, of any age, seldom cry, and when they do it is a kind of howl; when hurt or punished, they very rarely shed tears, or sob, but keep up a monotonous noise, which would never be imagined to be the crying of a child, but rather a song.

I once saw, in one of the market-places in Loanda, a boy of about sixteen lying on the ground, nearly naked, with his face and body covered with flies, but none of the busy thronging crowd had thought that he was dead and stiff, as I discovered when I touched him with my foot, but thought he was simply asleep and basking in the sun: his being covered with flies was too trivial a circumstance to attract any attention.

The manner in which negroes receive most severe wounds, with apparently little pain and absence of nervous shock, is most extraordinary. I have often been told of this by the Portuguese surgeons, who remark the absence of shock to the system with which negroes undergo amputations and other severe operations (without chloroform), which are attended by so much danger to the white race. I was staying at Ambrizzette when a man came there with his right hand blown to a mass of shreds, from the explosion of a gun-barrel; he was accompanied by his relatives, who took him to the different factories to beg the white men to cut off the hanging shreds of flesh and dress the injured part. All refused to attend to the man, till a Frenchman gave them a sharp razor, arnica, and balsam, and some bandages, and made them go out of the house and enclosure to operate on the sufferer themselves, away from the factories; which they did. About an hour after I was passing a group of natives sitting round a fire, and amongst them was the wounded man laughing and joking quite at his ease, and with his left hand roasting ground-nuts with the rest, as if nothing had happened to him.

The reason the white men refused to help the wounded black was not from want of charity or pity, as all would have done everything in their power to alleviate his sufferings, but it was the singular custom of the natives that prevented their doing so. Had he died, the white man who ministered to him would have been made responsible for his death, and would have been almost as heavily fined as if he had murdered him! If he got well, as he did, his benefactor would have been inconvenienced by heavy demands for his maintenance and clothing, and expected to make presents to the king, &c., for he would be looked upon as having saved his life, and consequently bound to support him, to a certain extent, as he was, though alive, unable from the accident to get his own living as readily as if he were uninjured. The Frenchman got over this risk by giving the remedies, not to the wounded black himself, but to his friends, and also making them clear out of the precincts of the house; so that in no case, whether the man died or lived, could any claim be made against him.

The only way to put a stop to the awful bloodshed now going on in the interior would be to organize an emigration scheme, under the direct supervision of the several governments who have entered into treaties for the abolition of slavery, and transport the poor wretches, now being murdered in cold blood by thousands, to tropical climates where they might earn their living by the cultivation of those articles necessary for consumption in civilized countries; their constitution would enable them to resist the climate, and they would gradually become civilized.

One great bar to their civilization in Angola, is that no tribe on the coast can be induced to work for wages, except as servants in houses and stores, and even these are mostly slaves of other natives, or work to pay off some fine or penalty incurred in their towns. For some years that I have been collecting the inner bark of the Adansonia digitata, or Baobab tree (the application of which to paper-making I discovered in 1858, and commenced working as a commercial speculation in 1865), I have been unable to induce one single native to hire himself to work by day or piecework; they will cut, prepare, and dry it, and bring it for sale, but nothing will induce them to hire themselves, or their slaves, to a white man.

There are at present in Angola several sugar and cotton plantations worked by slaves, called at present "libertos," who are meant by the Portuguese Government to work ten years, as a compensation to their owners for the capital expended in their purchase and for their clothing, education and medical treatment. At a near date, the total abolition of slavery in Angola has been decreed, and will come into force; with the inevitable result of the ruin of the plantations, or of its becoming a dead letter in the province.

By the native laws, a black once sold as a slave, and escaping back to his tribe, is considered a free man, so that a planter at present has no hold on his slaves; if they escape into the neighbouring towns, the natives will only deliver them up on the payment of a certain amount, very often more than he had cost in the first instance.

No amount of kindness or good done to a negro will have the slightest influence in preventing him from leaving his benefactor without as much as a "good-bye," or a shadow of an excuse, and very often going from a pampered existence to the certainty of the hard fare and life of their free condition, and this, not from the slightest idea of love of freedom, or anything of the kind, but simply from an animal instinct to live a lazy and vegetative existence.

When I was at Cuio, working a copper deposit, a black called Firmino, the slave of a Portuguese there, attached himself very much to me, and was, seemingly, never so happy as when accompanying me in my trips and rambles, and not from any payment I gave him, beyond a small and occasional present. When his master was leaving the place, Firmino came crying to me, begging me to buy him, that he might remain in my service as my slave, promising that he would never leave me.

His master generally treating him with harshness, if not cruelty, I took pity on him, and gave 13*l.* 10*s.* for him, a high and fancy price there, but he was considered worth it from his great size and strength, his speaking Portuguese perfectly, and good qualities generally.

I explained to him that although I had bought him, he was a free man, and could go at once if he liked; but that as long as he remained in my service as my personal attendant, he should have clothes and pay. He went on his knees to thank me and to swear in negro fashion, by making a cross in the dust with his forefinger, that he would never leave me. A fortnight after, having to send him with a bundle of clothes from Benguella to Cuio, he delivered them to the person they were addressed to, but joined three slaves in stealing a boat and sailing to Loanda.

A month after I received a letter from the police there advising me that a nigger called Firmino had been caught with others in an extensive robbery, and claimed to be my slave. I answered that he was no slave of mine, detailing the circumstances of my freeing him, and asking that he should be dealt with as he deserved. He was punished and drafted as a soldier at Loanda, and on my meeting him there one day and asking him his reason for leaving me, and treating me so ungratefully, he said that "he did not know why he had done so;" and I do not believe he did, or ever tried to find out, or bothered his head any more about it.

It is no use disguising the fact that the negro race is, mentally, differently constituted from the white, however disagreeable and opposed this may be to the usual and prevailing ideas in this country. I do not believe, and I fearlessly assert, that there is hardly such a thing possible as the sincere conversion of a single negro to Christianity whilst in Africa, and under the powerful influence of their fellows. No progress will be made in the condition of the negro as long as the idea prevails that he can be reasoned out of his ignorance and prejudices, and his belief in fetish, or that he is the equal of the white man; in fact, he must remain the same as he is now, until we learn to know him properly, and what he really is.

Loanda was discovered in the year 1492, and since 1576 the white race has never abandoned it. The Jesuits and other missionaries did wonders in their time, and the results of their great work can be still noticed to this day: thousands of the natives, for 200 miles to the interior, can read and write very fairly, though there has hardly been a mission or school, except in a very small way, at Loanda itself, for many many years; but those accomplishments are all that civilization or example has done amongst them. They all believe firmly in their fetishes and charms, and though generally treated with the utmost kindness and equality by the Portuguese, the negro race, and even the mulattoes, have never advanced further than to hold secondary appointments, as writers or clerks, in the public offices and shops, and to appear (in public) in the most starched and dandyfied condition. I can only recollect one black man who had at all distinguished himself in trade; keeping low and filthy grog-shops being about the extent of their business capacity. Another honourable exception is a Captain Dias, who is the captain or governor of the district of the "Barra do Bengo," near Loanda, a very intelligent man, and from whom I several times experienced great kindness and hospitality.

PLATE II.
PORTO DA LENHA.

CHAPTER IV.
THE RIVER CONGO—BANANA—PORTO DA LENHA—BOMA—MUSSURONGO TRIBE—PIRATES—MUSHICONGO TRIBE—FISH—PALM CHOP—PALM WINE.

At the mouth of the River Congo and on its north bank a long spit of sand separates the sea from a small creek or branch of the river. On this narrow strip, called Banana, are established several factories, belonging to Dutch, French, and English houses, and serving principally as depôts for their other factories higher up the river and on the coast. The Dutch house especially is a large establishment, and it was in one of their small steamers that my wife and myself ascended the river in February 1873.

The first place we touched at was Porto da Lenha, about forty or forty-five miles from Banana. The river banks up to this point are sheer walls of large mangrove trees rising out of the water; at high water, particularly, hardly a dry place can be seen where one could land from a boat or canoe. The natives have, of course, openings known to themselves, under and through the mangrove, where their little canoes dart in and out.

Porto da Lenha (Plate II.) consists of half-a-dozen trading factories, built on ground enclosed from the river by piles, forming quays in front, where large vessels can discharge and load close alongside. The wharves are continually sinking, and have to be replaced by constant addition of new piles and layers of thick fresh-water bivalve shells, very abundant in the river. We here found growing in the mud, and with the roots covered by the river at high water, the lovely orchid "*Lissochilus giganteus*" in full bloom; we collected some of its roots, which reached England safely, and are now growing in Kew Gardens. Several fine creepers were also in flower, and we observed numerous butterflies, which were not easy to capture from the difficulty of getting at them, as at the back of the houses the dense bush grows out of swamp, and only those specimens crossing the small dry space on which the houses are built could be collected. Little creeks divide one house from another; in some cases a plank bridge affords communication, but it is mostly effected by boats. A few days before our arrival a flood had covered the whole of the ground with several inches of water. Considering the conditions of the place, it does not seem to be so unhealthy to Europeans as might be expected. Next day we proceeded to Boma, also situated on the north bank of the river, about ninety-five miles from Banana.

The scenery completely changes after leaving Porto da Lenha, the mangrove totally disappears, and several kinds of bright green bushes, interspersed with different palms and trees, cover the banks for many miles. Near Boma, however, the banks are higher, and become bare of trees and shrubs, the whole country being comparatively free of any other vegetation but high grass; we have arrived, in fact, at the grass-covered high country before mentioned as beginning at the third elevation from the coast over the whole of Angola.

We were most hospitably received by a young Portuguese, Senhor Chaves, in charge of an English factory there, picturesquely situated, overlooking the banks of the river. A high hill opposite Boma and across the river is covered from the top right down to the water's edge with an impenetrable forest, and it is not easy to explain this vegetation, as it stands in such singular relief to the comparative barrenness of the surrounding country, gigantic Baobabs being the great tree-feature of the place. We crossed the river several times to this thickly-wooded hill, and were only able to find just sufficient shore to land under the branches of the trees, one of which (*Lonchocarpus sericeus*) was in beautiful bloom. The current of the river is so strong, and the stream so broad, that it took us half-an-hour to get across in a good boat with ten strong Kroomen paddling.

The view from a high hill on the north bank is magnificent: a succession of bends of the river, and as far as the sight could reach, the flat country to the south and west cut into innumerable islands and creeks, of the brightest green of the water-grass and papyrus reed, divided by the sunlit and quicksilver-like streams of the vast rapidly-flowing river.

Boma, as before observed, was formerly the great slave-trade mart, thousands arriving from all quarters of the interior; they generally carried a load of provisions, chiefly small beans, a species of the haricot, for sale to the traders, and on which the slaves were chiefly fed, in the barracoons and on board the vessels in which they were shipped, and the Congo used in this way to supply the coast, even to Loanda, with abundance of beans, mandioca-meal, &c.; but since the cessation of the slave-trade there has been such great scarcity of native grown food produce, not only in the river but everywhere on the coast—the cultivation of other products, such as ground-nuts, being of greater advantage to the natives—that Europeans are sometimes reduced to great straits for food for the natives in their service, and even for the fowls. This is one of the curious changes produced in the country by the abolition of the slave-trade. A very large trade quickly sprang up at Boma in ground-nuts, palm-oil, palm-kernels, &c.; but a foolish competition amongst the white traders has induced them to go higher up the river to trade; the consequence has been that Boma, so capitally situated in every way for a trading station, is now nearly reduced to a depôt for produce brought from farther up the river.

We were a fortnight at Boma, but were greatly disappointed at the small number of species of insects we collected, and the poverty in plants as well.

All the lovely coloured finches and other birds of the grassy regions were here most conspicuous in number and brilliancy, and it was really beautiful to see the tall grass alive with the brightest scarlet, yellow, orange, and velvet black of the many different species, at that season in their full plumage.

We were very much amused at a pretty habit of the males of the tiny little sky-blue birds (*Estrelda cyanogastra*) that, with other small birds such as the Spermestes, Estreldas, Pytelias, &c., used to come down in flocks to feed in the open space round the house. The little mites would take a grass flower in their beaks, and perform quite a hoppy dance on any little stick or bush, bobbing their feathery heads up and down, whilst their tiny throats swelled with the sweetest little song-notes and trills imaginable. This was their song to the females, who were feeding about on the ground below them. The long-tailed little whydah birds (*Vidua principalis*) have a somewhat similar habit of showing off whilst the hens are feeding on the ground; they keep hovering in the air about three or four feet above them, twit-twitting all the time, their long tails rising and falling most gracefully to the up-and-down motion of their little bodies.

One Sunday during our stay Senhor Chaves organized a pic-nic of the principal white traders to a native village in the interior, where he had arranged that the nine kings who govern Boma and receive "customs" from the traders, should meet us, in order that he might make them each a "dash," which he wished my wife to present, in commemoration of a white woman's visit. We started in hammocks, and after about two hours' journey, arrived at the place of meeting, where a good breakfast awaited us. Our road was over hilly ground, rough and rocky (mica schist), and was remarkably bare of vegetation; we passed one or two large and well-cultivated ravines.

After breakfast the nine kings appeared on the scene, and a miserable lot they were, with one exception, a fine tall old grizzly negro; their retinues were of the same description, and wretchedly clad. There was a big palaver, the customary amount of rum was consumed by them, and they each received, from my wife, their "dress" of several yards of cloth, piece of cotton handkerchiefs, red baize sash, and red cotton nightcap. One old fellow had a very curious old crucifix, which he did not know the age of; he could only tell that he was the fifth Soba or king that had inherited it. It had evidently belonged to the old Catholic Portuguese missionaries of former times.

Crucifixes are often seen as "fetishes" of the kings in Angola. Nothing will induce them to part with them, as they belong to part of the "fetishes" that have been handed down from king to king from time immemorial, and must not be lost or disposed of.

An amusing incident occurred on our way at a large village, where a great crowd, chiefly of women and children, had collected to cheer the white woman, seen for the first time in their lives. My hammock was a little way behind, and on arriving at the village I was met with great shouts and much shaking of hands; as the other white men had not been similarly received, I inquired the reason why, and was then informed that it was to denote their satisfaction at seeing the "proprietor or owner of the white woman," as they expressed it.

The natives here, in fact above Porto da Lenha, are Mushicongos, and are not a bad set of blacks; but, like all this large tribe, are weak and puny in appearance, dirty in their habits, and scanty of clothing. They have not as yet allowed white men to pass from Boma, or any other point of the river, to St. Salvador, and several Portuguese who have wished to go from St. Salvador to Boma have been dissuaded from attempting the journey by the king and natives, not from any objection on their part, but from the certainty that the blacks near the river would make them turn back.

There is a very great objection on the part of all the tribes of the interior of Angola, and particularly of those not in the actual territory held by the Portuguese, to the passage of a white man through the country. This is due in the first place to the natural distrust and suspicion of the negro character, and secondly to their fear of the example of the occupation of Ambriz and the Bembe mines by the Portuguese. It is impossible for blacks to understand that a white man will travel for curiosity's sake; it is perfectly incomprehensible to them that he should spend money in carriers, making presents, &c., only for the pleasure of seeing the country; they are never satisfied without what they consider a good reason; consequently they always imagine it must be for the purpose of establishing a factory for trade, or else to observe the country for its occupation thereafter. This is the reason why natives will never give reliable information regarding even the simplest question of direction of roads, rivers, distances, &c. It is very difficult to obtain exact information, and it is only after being very well acquainted with them that their natural suspicions are lulled, and they will freely afford the knowledge desired.

Their explanations of our object in collecting insects, birds, and other objects of natural history were very curious. Our statements that we did so to show in the white man's country what plants, insects, birds, &c., were to be found in Africa, as ours were so different, never satisfied them; they always thought that the specimens must be worth a great deal of money amongst the white men, or, as others did not devote themselves to collecting, it was to make "fetishes" of them when we got home: some, who considered themselves wiser than the others, said it was to copy designs for the Manchester prints, and that they would see the flowers, butterflies, and birds, copied on the trade cloth as soon as I got back to my country.

Their idea of my manufacturing the specimens into "fetishes" was a perfectly natural one in my case, as my nickname at Ambriz and on the coast is "Endoqui," or fetish man, from my having introduced the new trade of collecting and pressing the bark of the Adansonia tree, and from my wonderful performances in working a small steam engine, and putting up the hydraulic presses and a corrugated iron store, the first they had seen, and which caused great surprise.

The natives of the Congo River, from its mouth to a little above Porto da Lenha, belong to the Mussurongo tribe, and are an ill-favoured set—they are all piratical robbers, never losing an opportunity of attacking a loaded barge or even ship, unless well armed or keeping in the centre of the river, where the great current prevents them from collecting around it in their canoes. These pirates have been continually attacked by the Portuguese and English men-of-war, generally after some more than usually daring robbery, and have had several severe thrashings, but without their taking the slightest example by them, the next ship or boat that runs aground on the numerous sandbanks being again immediately attacked. They have taken several white men prisoners on such occasions, and have exacted a ransom for their liberation. They have, however, always treated them well whilst detained in their towns. The principal houses now do their trade by steamers, which the Mussurongos dare not, of course, attack.

A few years ago, a notorious pirate chief called Manoel Vacca, who had caused great loss to the traders by his piracy, was captured by them at Porto da Lenha and delivered to the British Commodore, who, instead of hanging him at the yard-arm as he deserved, and as an example to the nest of thieves of which he was the chief, took him to St. Helena, and after some time brought this savage back carefully to Porto da Lenha to his disconsolate followers, who had been unable to find a fit leader for their piratical robberies. Manoel Vacca, of course, quickly forgot his promises of amendment made whilst on board the British man-of-war, and again became the pest he had formerly been, and when we were up the river had exacted, without the slightest pretence but that of revenge, a large payment from the traders at Porto da Lenha, threatening to stop all trade, rob all boats, and kill the "cabindas" or crews, on the river, if not immediately paid, and—on our way from Boma—we narrowly escaped being involved in a fight there, in consequence of this scandalous demand, which I afterwards heard had been complied with. The traders vowed that if ever they caught him again, they would not deliver him to have his education continued at St. Helena, but would finish it on the spot.

The Mussurongos are very fond of wearing ankle-rings, which, when of brass, are Birmingham made, and obtained from the traders, but in many cases are made by the natives of iron forged by their smiths, and cast-tin or pewter, which they obtain in trade in the form of little bars. Those made by the natives are invariably ornamented with one peculiar design (Plate IV.). These rings are seldom above a few ounces in weight, and are worn by men and women alike, very different from the natives of Cabinda, on the north of the River Congo, whose women wear them as large and heavy as they can be made. I have in my possession two copper ankle-rings which I purchased for six shawl-handkerchiefs of a little old Cabinda woman at Ambriz, weighing seven pounds each. It cost a smith some considerable time and trouble to take them off, as from their thickness it was very difficult to wedge them open without injury to the woman's legs. It seems almost incredible that Fashion should, even among these uncivilized tribes, compel the dark sex to follow her arbitrary exactions, to the extent of carrying the enormous weight of fourteen pounds of solid metal on their naked feet. Till the ankles become hardened and used to the rings, the wearers are obliged to tie rags round them, to protect the skin from injury by the heavy weight.

The River Congo teems with animal life: above Porto da Lenha hippopotami are very abundant; alligators, of course, swarm, and are very dangerous.

Of the few small fish that I caught with a line at Boma, no less than four were new species, and have been named by Dr. A. Günther, of the British Museum, as the Bryconœthiops microstoma, Alestes holargyreus, Distichodus affinis, and Mormyrus Monteiri (see 'Annals and Magazine of Natural History' for August, 1873).

At Boma the Koodoo (*Tragelaphus Spekei*, Sclater) antelope must be very abundant, judging from the number of times that we there ate of its delicious flesh, brought in for sale by the natives. In my former visits to Banana I made several shooting excursions to neighbouring villages of friendly natives, in company with a Portuguese called Chico, employed at the Dutch factory, who was a keen sportsman: we generally started in the evening, and slept at a village a few miles off, rising at daybreak to shoot wild fowl in the lovely creeks and marshes, before the sun forced us to return to breakfast and the welcome shade of the palm-trees, under which were the pretty huts of the village.

Our breakfast invariably consisted of "palm chop," a delicious dish when properly prepared, and from the fresh nut. This dish has been so abused by travellers, who have perhaps hardly tasted it more than once, and who might have been prejudiced by the colour of the oil, or the idea that they were eating waggon-grease or palm-soap, that I must give an accurate description of its preparation and defend its excellence against its detractors. The nuts of the oil-palm (*Elæis Guineensis*) are about the size of large chestnuts, the inner part being excessively hard and stony, and containing an almond (technically "palm-kernel"). It is enclosed or surrounded by a thin outer mass of fibre and pulp containing the oil, and covered with a rich red-brown skin or husk somewhat thinner than that on a chestnut. The pulpy oil and fibrous portion being separated from the nuts, is melted in a pot over the fire to further separate all the fibres, and the rich, thick oily mass is then ready to be added to a dismembered duck or fowl, or any other kind of meat, and the whole stewed gently together with the proper amount of water, with the addition of ground green Chili peppers and salt to taste, until it is quite done, and in appearance like a rich curry, with which it can best be compared; a squeeze of lime or lemon is a great improvement. The flavour of this dish is not at all like what might be expected from the strong smell of the often rancid palm oil received in this country. It is always eaten with some boiled preparation of maize flour, or better still of meal from the mandioca root. A good cook will make a very good "palm chop" with fresh oil, in the absence of the new nuts.

Another excellent dish is the ordinary haricot bean stewed with palm oil and Chili peppers till quite tender and thick.

It is from the oil-palm that the finest palm wine is obtained, and it is curious how few travellers have accurately described this or its properties. The blacks ascend the trees by the aid of a ring formed of a stout piece of the stem of a creeper which is excessively strong and supple: one end is tied into a loop, and the other thrown round the tree is passed through the loop and bent back (Plate IV.): the end being secured forms a ready and perfectly safe ring, which the operator passes over his waist. The stumps of the fallen leaves form projections which very much assist him in getting up the tree. This is done by taking hold of the ring with each hand, and by a succession of jerks, the climber is soon up at the top, with his empty gourds hung round his neck. With a pointed instrument he taps the tree at the crown, and attaches the mouth of a gourd to the aperture, or he takes advantage of the grooved stem of a leaf cut off short to use as a channel for the sap to flow into the gourd suspended below. This operation is performed in the evening, and in the early morning the gourds are brought down with the sap or juice that has collected in them during the night. The palm wine is now a slightly milky fluid, in appearance as nearly as possible like the milk in the ordinary cocoa-nut, having very much the same flavour, only sweeter and more luscious.

When cool in the morning, as brought down fresh from the tree, it is perfectly delicious, without the slightest trace of fermentation, and of course not in the least intoxicating; in a few hours, or very shortly if collected or kept in old gourds in which wine has previously fermented, it begins to ferment rapidly, becoming acid and intoxicating; not so much from the quantity of alcohol produced, I believe, as from its being contained in a strongly effervescent medium, and being drunk by the natives in the hot time of the day, and when they are heated by travelling, &c. Even in the morning the wine has sometimes a slightly acid flavour, if it has been collected in an old calabash. We used to have new gourds employed for ourselves. The natives, again, can never be trusted to bring it for sale perfectly fresh or pure, always mixing it with water or old wine, and of course spoiling it, and I have known the rascals take water in the calabashes up the tree to mix with the pure juice, when they thought they should not have an opportunity of adulterating it before selling it.

PLATE III.
VIEW ON THE CONGO, ABOVE BOMA.

The smell of the palm wine, as it dries on the tree tops where they have been punctured, is very attractive to butterflies, bees, wasps, and other insects, and these in their turn attract the many species of insectivorous birds. This is more particularly the case with the beautiful little sunbirds (*Nectariniæ*), always seen in numbers busily employed in capturing their insect prey, actively flitting, from top to top, and darting in and out of the leaf-stems with a little song very much like that of the cock-robin.

CHAPTER V.
COUNTRY FROM THE RIVER CONGO TO AMBRIZ—VEGETATION—TRADING—CIVILIZATION—COMMERCE—PRODUCTS—IVORY—MUSSERRA—SLEEP DISEASE—SALT—MINERAL PITCH.

The southern point, at the entrance of the River Congo, is called Point Padrão, from a marble "Padrão," or monument raised by the Portuguese to commemorate the discovery of the River Congo by Diogo Cam, in 1485. At a short distance from it there formerly existed a monastery and missionary establishment dedicated to Santo Antonio. That part of the southern bank of the river opposite Banana is called Santo Antonio to this day, and a few years ago a Portuguese trader opened a house there for the purpose of trade; in this he was followed by the agent of a Liverpool firm, but the result, naturally to be foreseen, took place, and both factories were robbed and burnt down by the rascally Mussurongos. Some time before this took place, I was waiting at Banana for some means of conveyance by sea to Ambriz, but none appearing, I determined, in company with a Brazilian who was also desirous of proceeding to the same place, to cross over to Santo Antonio, and try if we could induce the natives to allow us to pass thence over land to Cabeça da Cobra. This we did, and remained at the trader's house till we got carriers and permission, on making a small present to the king of Santo Antonio town, to pass through. No white man had been allowed to do so for many years.

We started one night as soon as the moon rose, about one o'clock, and after travelling a couple of hours, almost the whole time over marshy ground and through a dry wood, which we had to pass on foot,—as it was a fetish wood and it would have been highly unlucky to cross it in our hammocks,—we arrived at the town of Santo Antonio, which appeared large and well populated. Here we rested for a little while, whilst we got some fresh carriers, and the king and several of the natives came to see us and received two pieces of cotton handkerchiefs, and a couple of gallons of rum, which we had brought for them. The old bells of the monastery are still preserved in the town, hung from trees, and we were treated with a din on them in return for our present. We then continued our journey over good dry ground till we arrived at Cabeça da Cobra, or "Snake's Head," in time for a late breakfast at the house of a Portuguese trader. Here Senhor Fernando José da Silva presented me with a letter of introduction he had brought with him from Lisbon some years previously, and which he had not before had an opportunity of delivering.

I at once engaged him to help me in developing my discovery of the application of the fibre of the Baobab (*Adansonia digitata*) to paper-making, and in introducing among the natives the new industry of collecting and preparing it, and I must here render him a tribute of gratitude for his friendship and the unceasing activity and energy with which he has laboured to assist me in permanently establishing this new trade, in the face of the greatest difficulties, privations, and hard work for long years on the coast.

The coast line from Cabeça da Cobra to Ambriz is principally composed of red bluffs and cliffs, and the road or path is generally near the edge of the cliffs, affording fine views of the sea and surf-beaten beach below. The country is arid and thinly wooded, and is covered with hard, wiry, branched grass; and the curious Mateba palm grows in great abundance in the country from the River Congo to Moculla, where it is replaced by the Cashew tree as far as Ambrizzette. The flat-leaved Sansevieria (*S. longiflora*) is extremely abundant, and disappears south almost entirely about Musserra, where it is in its turn replaced by Sansevieria Angolensis. These changes are very curious and striking, being so well marked on a comparatively small extent of coast. The Baobab tree is everywhere seen, its vast trunk throwing, by comparison, all other trees into insignificance: it is less abundant perhaps from the River Congo to about Ambrizzette; from that place, southwards, the country is one open forest of it.

The natives as far as Mangue Grande are Mussurongos. From this to Ambriz they are a branch of the Mushicongo tribe. The Mussurongos are at present an indolent set, but there are signs that they are becoming more industrious, now that they have given up all hope of seeing the slave-trade again established, which enabled them, as one said to me, to be rich without working. Since the last slave was shipped from this part of the coast, about the year 1868, the development of produce in the country itself and from the interior has been very great indeed, and promises in a few years to be still more, and very important in amount. This will be more particularly the case when the present system ceases, by which the natives of the coast towns act as middle-men to the natives from the interior. At present nearly the entire bulk of the produce comes from the interior, no extensive good plantation grounds being found before arriving at the first elevation, which we have seen to commence at from thirty to sixty miles from the coast, the ivory coming from not less than 200 to 300 miles.

The blacks, on arriving from the interior, put up at the towns on the coast, where the natives, having been in constant intercourse with the whites for years, all speak Portuguese, and many of them English. It is a fact that the natives speak Portuguese more correctly than they do English, which I attribute to the good custom of the Portuguese very seldom stooping to murder their language when speaking to the blacks, which the English universally do, under the mistaken idea of rendering themselves more intelligible.

These blacks act as interpreters and brokers, and are thereby enabled to satisfy fully and successfully their innate propensity for roguery by cheating the natives from the interior to their hearts' content. They bargain the produce with the white men at one price, telling the natives always that it is for a much lower sum, of course pocketing the difference, sometimes amounting to one-half and more. It is a common thing to be asked to have only so much,—naming the amount for which they have pretended to have sold the produce,—paid whilst the owners are present, and getting a "book" or ticket for the rest, which they receive from the white trader at another time.

It has been found impossible to do away with this custom, as the white men are almost dependent for their trade upon these rogues, called "linguisteres" (derived evidently from the Portuguese term "lingoa," "tongue," or interpreter). These have their defence for the custom, first, that it has always existed, a great argument with the conservative negro race; secondly, that it is their commission for looking after the interests of the natives from the interior, who would otherwise be cheated by the white men, who would take advantage of their want of knowledge of the selling prices on the coast; and thirdly that they have to make presents to the natives out of these gains, and give them drink at the towns to keep them as their customers and prevent their going to other towns or linguisteres. The natives from the interior, again, are very suspicious and afraid of the white man, and they would hardly dare approach him without being under the protection of the coast negroes. There is no doubt that the development of the trade from the interior would increase greatly if the natives and owners of the produce obtained the full price paid by the white men. There is almost a certainty, however, that the system will not last much longer, as the natives are beginning to find out how they are cheated by their coast brethren, and are already, in many cases, trading direct with the white men.

The system adopted in trading or bartering with the natives on the coast, comprehended between the River Congo and Ambriz, is somewhat complicated and curious. All produce (except ivory) on being brought to the trader, is put on the scales and the price is agreed, in "longs" in English, or "peças" in Portuguese. This "peça" or "long" is the unit of exchange to which all the multifarious articles of barter are referred: for instance, six yards of the ordinary kinds of cotton cloth, such as stripes, unbleached calico, blue prints, cotton checks, are equal to a "long;" a yard and a half of red or blue baize, five bottles of rum, five brass rods, one cotton umbrella, 3000 blue glass beads, three, six, eight, or twelve cotton handkerchiefs, according to size and quality, are also severally equal to a "long;" articles of greater value, such as kegs of powder, guns, swords, knives, &c., are two or more "longs" each.

As each bag of coffee (or other produce) is weighed and settled for, the buyer writes the number of "longs" that has been agreed upon on a small piece of paper called by the natives "Mucanda," or, by those who speak English, a "book;" the buyer continues his weighing and purchasing, and the "books" are taken by the natives to the store, which is fitted up like a shop, with shelves on which are arranged at hand the many different kinds of cloth, &c., employed in barter. The natives cannot be trusted in the shop, which contains only the white man and his "Mafuca" or head man, so the noisy, wrangling mob is paid from it through a small window. We will suppose, for instance, that a "book" is presented at the window, on which is marked twenty "longs" as the payment of a bag of coffee; the trader takes—

A gun—value	4 longs
One keg powder	2 "
One piece of 18 yards stripes	3 "
One of 18 yards grey calico	3 "
One of 18 yards checks	3 "
Eight handkerchiefs	1 "
Five bottles of rum	1 "
One table-knife	1 "
Three thousand beads	1 "
Five brass rods	1 "
Total:	20 longs.

This is now passed out, the trader making such alterations in the payment as the natives desire within certain limits, exchanging, for instance, the handkerchiefs for red baize, or the piece of calico for a sword, but there is an understanding that the payment is to be a certain selection, from which only small deviations can be made. If such were not the case the payment of 100 or more "books" in a short time would be impossible. It is by no means an easy task to trade quickly and successfully with the natives; long practice, and great patience and good temper are necessary. A good trader, who is used to the business, can pay the same "book" for a great deal less value than one unaccustomed to the work, and the natives will often refuse to trade with a new man or one not used to their ways and long known to them.

It is rather startling to a stranger to see and hear a couple of hundred blacks all shouting at the top of their voices to be paid first, and quarrelling and fighting over their payment, or pretending to be dissatisfied with it, or that they have been wrongly paid.

Ivory is purchased in a different manner; the tusk is weighed, and an offer made by the trader in guns, barrels of powder and "longs," generally in about the proportion of one gun, one keg of powder, and two longs; thus a tusk, we will say, is purchased for twelve guns, twelve kegs of powder, and twenty-four "longs." The natives do not receive this, but a more complicated payment takes place; of the twelve guns they only receive four, the rest being principally in cloth, on a scale well understood, the guns being calculated generally at four "longs" each; the same process is carried out with the kegs of powder, only a certain number being actually given in that commodity: the twenty-four "longs" are given in cloth and a variety of small objects, including razors, cheap looking-glasses, padlocks, ankle rings, playing-cards, empty bottles, hoop-iron off the bales, brass tacks, glass tumblers and decanters, different kinds of beads, &c. The amount first agreed upon is called the "rough bundle," and the trader, by adding the value of the guns, powder, and "longs," and dividing the sum by the weight of the tusk, can tell very nearly what the pound of ivory will cost when reduced by the substitution of the various numerous articles given in lieu of the guns and powder agreed upon on the purchase of the tusk.

The small extent of coast comprised between Ambriz and the River Congo is a striking example of the wonderful increase of trade, and consequently industry, among the negroes, since the extinction of the slave trade, and evidences also the great fertility of a country that with the rudest appliances can produce such quantities of valuable produce; about a dozen years ago, a very few tons, with the exception of ivory, of ground-nuts, coffee, and gum copal only, were exported. Last year the exports from Ambriz to, and not including, the River Congo, were as follows:—

Adansonia fibre	1500 tons
Ground-nuts	7500 "
Coffee	1000 "
Sesamum seed	650 "
Red gum copal	50 "
White Angola gum	100 "
India-rubber	400 "
Palm-kernel	100 "
Ivory	185 "

Besides this amount of produce, the value of which may be estimated at over 300,000*l*., a considerable quantity of ground-nuts find their way to the River Congo from the interior of the country I am now describing. This is already a most gratifying and interesting result, and one from which valuable lessons are to be deduced, when we come to compare it with what has taken place in other parts of the coast, most notably in the immediate neighbouring country to the south in the possession of the Portuguese, and is a splendid example of the true principles by which the African race *in Africa* can be successfully civilized, and the only manner in which the riches of the West Coast can be developed and made available to the wants of the rest of the world.

There can be no doubt that our attempts to civilize the negro by purely missionary efforts have been a signal failure. I will say more: so long as missionary work consists of simply denominational instruction and controversy, as at present, it is mischievous and retarding to the material and mental development and prosperity of Africa. Looking at it from a purely religious point of view, I emphatically deny that a single native has been converted, otherwise than in name or outward appearance, to Christianity or Christian morality. Civilization on the coast has certainly succeeded in putting a considerable number of blacks into uncomfortable boots and tight and starched clothes, and their women outwardly into grotesque caricatures of Paris fashions, as any one may witness by spending even only a few hours at Sierra Leone, for instance, where he will see the inoffensive native transformed into a miserable strutting bully, insolent to the highest degree, taught to consider himself the equal of the white man, as full as his black skin can hold of overweening conceit, cant, and hypocrisy, without a vice or superstition removed, or a virtue engrafted in his nature, and calling the native whose industry supplies him with food, "You nigga! Sah!"

This is the broad and characteristic effect of present missions on the coast, I am sorry to say, and they will continue to be fruitless as long as they are not combined with industrial training. That was the secret of the success of the old Catholic missionaries in Angola; they were traders as well, and taught the natives the industrial arts, gardening, and agriculture. What if they derived riches and power, the envy of which led to their expulsion, from their efforts, so long as they made good carpenters, smiths, masons, and other artificers of the natives, and created in them a new life, and the desire for better clothing, houses, and food, which they could only satisfy by work and industry?

On landing at Bonny from the steamer, to collect plants and insects on the small piece of dry land opposite the hulks in the river, we saw the pretty little church and schoolroom belonging to the mission there, in which were a number of children repeating together, over and over again, like a number of parrots, "I know dat I hab a soul, because I feel someting widin me." Only a few yards off was the village in which they lived, and a large fetish house exactly the same as any other; not a sign of work of any kind, not a square yard of ground cleared or planted, not a fowl or domestic animal, save a lean cur or two, to be seen; the children, and even big girls, or young women, in a complete state of nudity,—nothing in fact to show any difference whatever from any other town in the country. Can any one believe for a moment that the instruction afforded by that mission was of any avail, that the few irksome hours of repetition of texts, writing and reading, explanations of the Bible, &c., could in the least counteract the influence of the fetish house in the village, or the superstition and ignorance of the children's parents and elders, or remove the fears and prejudices imbibed with their mothers' milk? Is it not more natural to suppose, as is well known to be the case, that this imperfect training is just sufficient to enable them when older to be sharper, more dishonest and greater rogues than their fellows, and to ape the vices of the white man, without copying his virtues or his industry?

I remember at Ambrizzette a black who could read and write, forging a number of "books" for gunpowder, and thus robbing some of the houses to a considerable extent. The natives wanted to kill him, but on the white men interceding for his life, they chopped off the fingers of his right hand with a matchet, to prevent his forging any more. Educated blacks, or even mulattoes, cannot be trusted as clerks, with the charge of factories, or in other responsible situations. I do not remember a case in which loss did not sooner or later result from their employment.

Trade or commerce is the great civilizer of Africa, and the small part of the coast we are treating of at present is a proof of this. Commerce has had undisturbed sway for a few years, with the extraordinary result already stated. The natives have not been spoilt as yet by contact with the evils of an ignorant and oppressive occupation, as in Portuguese Angola, or, as on the British West Coast on the other hand, by having been preached by a dozen opposed and rival sects into a muddled state of assumed and insolent equality with the white race, whom they hate in their inmost hearts, from the consciousness of their infinite inferiority.

Commerce has spread before them a tempting array of Manchester goods, guns, gunpowder, blankets, rugs, coats, knives, looking-glasses, playing cards, rum and gin, matchets, tumblers and decanters, beads, silver and brass ankle-rings, and many other useful or ornamental articles, without any duties to pay, or any compulsory regulations of passports, papers, tolls, or hindrances of any kind; the only key necessary is a bag of produce on the scales; a fair, and in many cases, even high price is given in return, and every seller picks and chooses what he or she desires;—and let not rum or gin be abused for its great share in the development of produce, for it is a powerful incentive to work. A black dearly loves his drop of drink; he will very often do for a bottle of rum, what he would not even think of stirring for, for three times the value in any other article, and yet they are not great drunkards, as we shall see, when describing their customs; they so divide any portion of spirits they can obtain, that it does them no harm whatever. The rum and gin, though of the very cheapest description, is pure and unsophisticated, the only adulteration being an innocent one practised by the traders, who generally mix a liberal proportion of water with it.

When a black does give way to intemperate habits, his friends make him undergo "fetish" that he shall drink no more, and such is their dread of consequences if they do not keep their "fetish" promise, that I have known very few cases of their breaking the "pledge." Sometimes a black is "fetished" for rum or other spirit-drinking, but not against wine, which they are beginning to consume in increasing quantity; the kind they are supplied with being the ordinary red Lisbon.

In describing the different kinds of produce of this country, the first on the list, the inner bark of the "Baobab," or Adansonia digitata, claims precedence, it being the latest discovery of an African production as an article of commerce, and of great importance from its application to paper-making, and also from its opening a new and large field to native industry.

It was on my first arrival in Ambriz in February 1858, that this substance struck me as being fit for making good paper: a few simple experiments enabled me to make specimens of bleached fibre and pulp from it, proving to me conclusively its suitableness for that purpose.

Having been engaged in mining in Angola, it was not till the year 1865 that I finally determined to proceed to Ambriz, with the view of developing my discovery, and I have ever since been actively engaged in establishing houses on the part of the coast I am now describing, for bartering the Adansonia fibre,—pressing and shipping the same to England. In my long and arduous task I have met with more than the ordinary amount of losses and disappointments, from commercial failures and other causes that seem to fall to the lot of discoverers or inventors in general; but I have triumphed over all obstacles and prejudices, and have established its success as a paper-making material beyond any doubt.

The Baobab, or "monkey fruit tree," is well known from descriptions as one of the giants of the vegetable kingdom. It rears its vast trunk thirty or forty feet high, with a diameter of three or four feet in the baby plants, to usually twenty to thirty feet in the older trees. Adansonias of more than thirty feet in diameter are rare, but they have been measured of as great a size as over 100 feet in circumference; the thickest trunk I have ever seen was sixty-four feet in circumference, and was clean and unbroken, without a crack on its smooth bark.

The leaves and flowers are produced during the rainy season, and are succeeded by the long pendant gourd-like fruit, like hanging notes of admiration, giving the gigantic, nearly leafless tree a most singular appearance. Millions of these trees cover the whole of Angola, as they do in fact the whole of tropical Africa, sufficient to supply an incalculable amount of paper material for years, but for the indolence of the negro race. I have no doubt, however, that they will in time follow the example of the Ambriz blacks, and a very large trade be developed as in the case of the palm-oil and the india-rubber trade.

The leaves of the Baobab when young are good to eat, boiled as a vegetable, and in appearance are somewhat like a new horse-chestnut leaf about half grown, and of a bright green; the flowers are very handsome, being a large ball of pure white, about four or five inches across, exactly like a powder puff, with a crown of large thick white petals turned back on top of it. After a few days the flowers become tipped with yellow, before dropping from the tree. The trunks, even of the largest trees, have properly speaking no wood, that is to say, a plank could not be sawn out of it, or any work made from it;—a section of a trunk shows first a thin outer skin or covering of a very peculiar pinkish ashen white, somewhat like that of a silver birch, some appearing quite silvery against the colour of other trees and foliage; then there follows about an inch of substance like hard mangold wurzel with fibres, then the thick coat of fibrous inner bark, which readily separates; next, the young wood, very much like the inner bark, and lastly, layers of more woody texture, divided or separated by irregular layers of pith, the most woody parts having no more firmness than perfectly rotten mildewed pine wood, and breaking quite readily with a ragged and very fibrous fracture.

The centre of these vast trunks easily rots, and becomes hollow from the top, where the stem generally branches off laterally into two or three huge arms. This is taken advantage of by the Quissama blacks, who inhabit the south bank of the River Quanza, to use them as tanks to store rain water in against the dry season, as it is a country very destitute of water.

The hollow Baobabs are very seldom open from the sides; I only remember one large tree of this kind in which an aperture like a door gave admittance into the empty centre; this was in Cambambe, and the hollow was large enough for two of us to sit inside, with a small box between us for a table, and have our breakfast, and room to spare for our cook to attend on us. Whilst we were comfortably enjoying our meal in its grateful shade, our cook suddenly gave a shout and rushed out, crying "Nhoca, Nhoca," "Snake, Snake," and sure enough there was a fine fellow about four feet long over-head, quietly surveying our operations; a charge of shot settled this very quickly, and down he fell, a victim to his curiosity.

The inner bark of the Adansonia is obtained by first chopping off the softer outer bark of the tree with a matchet, and then stripping the inner bark in large sheets. The smaller trees produce the finest and softest fibre, and it is taken off all round the tree, which does not appear to suffer much injury. A fresh layer of bark grows, and is thick enough to take off in about six to eight years. The bark is only taken off the large trunks in places where the outer bark is smooth and free from knobs, &c. In the course of time, the trunk growing, shows the scar, high above the ground, of the place where the bark has been taken off years before. The layers of inner bark when cut are saturated with sap; the pieces are beaten with a stick to soften them, and shaken to get rid of some of the pithy matter attached to them. The bark is then dried in the sun, when it is ready for pressing into bales, and shipping.

This inner bark is put to a variety of uses by the natives. It is twisted into string and rope for all sorts of purposes, or used in strips to secure loads, and to tie the sticks, &c., in making their huts. Finer pieces are pulled out so as to resemble a coarse network, and the edges being sewn together, make handy bags for cotton, or gum, grain, &c.; and very strong bags are woven from thin strips, in which coffee and ground-nuts are brought down from Cazengo to the coast.

Several amusing incidents occurred on my introducing the trade in Baobab fibre among the natives. I had great difficulty at first in inducing them to take to it, but they soon saw the advantage of doing on a large scale what they had been accustomed to do for their own small necessities; their principal reason for suspicion about it was that it had never before been an article purchased by the white men; they would not believe it was for making paper, but thought it must be for making cloth, and one old fellow very sagely affirmed that it was to be used for making mosquito curtains, from the open texture of the finer samples. It was debated at the towns whether it should be allowed to be cut and sold, and finally agreed to, and the trade was fully established at Ambriz for several months, when a report spread amongst the natives that the object of my buying it was to make it into ropes to tie them up some fine day when they least expected it, and ship them on board the steamers as slaves. Such was the belief in this absurd idea that all the natives employed at the factories disappeared, and not a man, woman, or child appeared in Ambriz for several days, and the place was nearly starved out.

I had an old black as my head man of the name of "Pae Tomás" (Father Thomas) who was very much respected in the country; he had been with me for some years, and it took all his influence to get the natives to return to Ambriz and to bring in fibre again for sale.

Another instance of how any little variation from the usual state of things will excite the suspicions of these natives, even accustomed as they have been to contact with white men for many years, was the appearance at Ambriz of a four-masted steamer,—one of the Lisbon monthly line: such a thing as a "ship with four sticks" had never been seen before, and without waiting to inquire, every black ran away from Ambriz, and the same thing happened on her return from Loanda; it was only after repeated voyages that the natives lost their fear of her; they could give no other reason than that it had never been seen before, and that therefore it must be a signal for the white men to do something or other they could not understand.

It was not till some time after putting up and working the hydraulic press at Ambriz that I was able to go north and establish them at other places. I had to invite the King and Council of Musserra to come to Ambriz and see it at work, and convince them that it was quite an inoffensive machine, and could only squeeze the fibre into bales; only by this means could I get their leave to land one there and erect it and begin the trade, and I believe that had I not been already long known to them I should have been unable to do it so soon. They somehow had the idea that the cylinder was a great cannon, and might be fired off with gunpowder, and I might take the country from them with it, but they were reassured when they saw it had no touch-hole at the breech, and that it was set upright in the ground and worked by water.

At Kimpoaça, a neighbouring town was averse to one being landed there, but as I had obtained the leave of the king and the townspeople they felt bound to allow me to set it up, and for about a fortnight that the surf prevented its being landed the whole of the inhabitants were on the beach every day with loaded guns, to fight the other town, if necessary, as they had threatened forcible opposition to its being put up—it all went off quietly, however, but a couple of years after, the rains having failed to come down at the proper time, the fetish men declared that the "matari ampuena," or the "big iron," had fetished the rain and prevented its appearance.

The matter was discussed in the country at a meeting of the people of the neighbouring towns, and it was determined to destroy the press and throw it into the sea if it was found to be a "feiticeiro," or wizard. This was, of course, to be proved by the ordeal by poison, namely, by making it take "casca," the bark that I have already described as determining the innocence or guilt of any one accused of witchcraft; but this difficulty presented itself to their minds, that as the "big iron" had no stomach or insides, the "casca" could have no action, so after much deliberation it was resolved to get over the difficulty by giving the dose to a slave of the king, who represented the hydraulic press. Very luckily the poison acted as an emetic, and the press was proved innocent of bewitching the rain. After some time, the rains persisting in not coming down, the poor slave was again forced to take "casca," but with the same fortunate result,—the press was saved, and the natives have never again suspected it of complicity with evil spirits.

It was these hydraulic presses for baling the baobab fibre, at Ambriz and elsewhere, which more than anything else firmly established amongst the natives the name they had given me of "Endoqui ampuena," or, the great wizard. There is something to them so marvellous in the simple working of a lever at a distance, by a little water in a tank, that no rational explanation is possible to their minds,—it is simply a case of pure witchcraft.

The fruit of the baobab is like a long gourd, about fourteen to eighteen inches in length, covered by a velvety greenish-brown coating, and hanging by a stalk two to three feet long. It is filled inside with a curious dry, pulverulent, yellowish-red substance, in which the seeds, about the size of pigeon-beans, are imbedded. The seeds are pounded and made into meal for food in times of scarcity, and the substance in which they are embedded is also edible, but strongly and agreeably acid. This gourd-like fruit is often used for carrying water or storing salt, &c., the walls, or shell, being very hard and about a quarter of an inch thick. From its shape it makes a very convenient vessel for baling water out of a canoe, one end being cut slantwise, and it is used by the natives everywhere on the coast for this purpose.

The finest orchilla weed is found growing on the baobab trees near the coast, and the natives ascend the great trunks by driving pegs into them one above the other, and using them as steps to get to the branches. These trees are the great resort of the several species of doves so abundant in Angola, and their favourite resting-place on account of the many nooks and spaces on the monstrous trunks and branches in which they can conveniently build their flat nests and rear their young.

There is something peculiarly grand in the near appearance of these trees, and it is impossible to describe the sensation caused by these huge vegetable towers, that have braved in solitary grandeur the hot sun and storms of centuries; and very pleasant it is to lie down under the shade of one of these giants and listen to the soft, plaintive "coo—coo—coo" of the doves above, the only sound that breaks the noonday silence of the hot and dry untrodden solitude around.

A lowly plant, but perhaps the most important in native tropical African agriculture, the ground-nut (*Arachis hypogæa*), next deserves description. Many thousand tons of this little nut are grown on the whole West Coast of Africa, large quantities being exported to Europe,—principally to France,—to be expressed into oil. We have already seen what a great increase has taken place in the cultivation of this nut in the part of the coast I am now specially describing, and I believe that it is destined to be one of the most important oil-seeds of the future.

The native name for it is "mpinda" or "ginguba," and it is cultivated in the greatest abundance at a few miles inland from the coast, where the comparatively arid country is succeeded by better ground and climate. It requires a rich soil for its cultivation, and it is chiefly grown, therefore, in the bottoms of valleys, or in the vicinity of rivers and marshes. The plant grows from one to two feet high, with a leaf and habit very much like a finely-grown clover. The bright-yellow pea-like flowers are borne on long slender stalks; these, after flowering, curl down, and force the pod into the ground, where it ripens beneath the soil. Its cultivation is a very simple affair. The ground being cleared, the weeds and grass are allowed to dry, and are then burnt; the ground is then lightly dug a few inches deep by the women with their little hoes—their only implement of agriculture—and the seeds dropped into the ground and covered up. The sowing takes place in October and November, at the beginning of the rainy season, and the first crop of nuts for eating green is ready about April; but they are not ripe for nine months after sowing, or about July or August, when they are first brought down to the coast for trade.

A large plantation of ground-nuts is a very beautiful sight: a rich expanse of the most luxuriant foliage of the brightest green, every leaf studded with diamond-like drops glittering in the early sun. The ground-nut is an important part of the food of the natives, and more so in the country from Ambriz to the River Congo than south at Loanda and Benguella. It is seldom eaten raw, but roasted, and when young and green, and roasted in the husks, is really delicious eating. It is excessively oily when fully ripe, and the natives then generally eat it with bananas and either the raw mandioca root, or some preparation of it, experience showing them the necessity of the admixture of a farinaceous substance with an excessively oily food. The nuts are also ground on a stone to a paste, with which to thicken their stews and messes. This paste, mixed with ground Chili pepper, is also made into long rolls, enveloped in leaves of the *Phrynium ramosissimum*, and is eaten principally in the morning to stay the stomach in travelling till they reach the proper camping-places for their breakfast or first meal and rest, generally about noon. It is called "quitaba," and I shall never forget the first time I tasted this composition: I thought my palate and tongue were blistered, so great was the proportion of Chili pepper in it.

A considerable quantity of oil used to be prepared by the natives from this nut by the most rudimentary process it is possible to imagine. The nuts are first pounded into a mass in a wooden mortar; a handful of this is then taken between the palms of the hands, and an attendant pours a small quantity of hot water on it, and on squeezing the hands tightly together the oil and water run out. Since the great demand for, and trade in, the ground-nut, but little oil is prepared by the natives, as they find it more advantageous to sell the nuts than to extract the oil from them by the wasteful process I have just described. Ground-nut oil is very thin and clear, and is greatly used in cookery in Angola, for which it is well adapted as it is almost free from taste and smell.

The greater part of the several thousand tons of nuts that at present constitute the season's crop in this part of the country is grown in the Mbamba country, lying parallel with the coast, at a distance of from thirty to eighty miles inland, or at the first and second elevation. Some idea of the great population of this comparatively small district may be formed from the fact that the whole of the above ground-nuts are shelled by hand, and brought down to the coast on the heads of the natives. It is difficult for any one unacquainted with the subject to realise the vast amount of labour implied in the operation of shelling this large quantity by hand.

The trade in coffee is almost entirely restricted to Ambriz, and it comes principally from the district of Encoge, a considerable quantity also being brought from the Dembos country and from Cazengo, to the interior of Loanda, from which latter place the trade is shut out by the stupid and short-sighted policy of high custom-house duties on goods, and other restrictions on trade of the Portuguese authorities. Very little of the coffee produced in the provinces of Encoge and Dembos is cultivated; it is the product of coffee-trees growing spontaneously in the virgin forests of the second elevation. The natives, of course, have no machinery of any kind to separate the berry from the pod, these being dried in the sun and then broken in a wooden mortar, and the husks separated by winnowing in the open air.

The sesamum seed (*Sesamum indicum*) has only very recently become an article of trade in Angola. It was cultivated sparingly by the natives, who employ it, ground to a paste on a stone in the same manner as the ground-nut, to add to their other food in cooking. It is as yet cultivated for trade principally by the natives about Mangue Grande, and only since about the year 1868, but there is no doubt it will be an important product all over Angola, as it is found to grow near the coast, in soil too arid for the ground-nut.

The red gum copal, called "maquata" by the natives, is of the finest quality, and is almost entirely the product of the Mossulo country. It is known to exist north, in the vicinity of Mangue Grande, but it is "fetish" for the natives to dig it, and consequently they will not bring it for trade, and even refuse to tell the exact place where it is found, but there can be no doubt about it, as they formerly traded in it with the white men.

Until about the year 1858, it was a principal article of export from Ambriz; vessels being loaded with it, chiefly to America, but with the American war the trade ceased, and it has never since attained anything like its former magnitude. I believe it to be a fossil gum or mineral resin. I have examined quantities of it, to discover any trace of leaves, insects, or other remains, that might prove it to have been of vegetable origin, but in vain.

It is obtained from a part of Angola where white men are not permitted by the natives to penetrate, and I have consequently not been an actual observer of the locality in which it occurs; but by all the accounts received from intelligent natives, it is found below the surface of a highly ferruginous hard clay or soil, at a depth of a few inches to a couple of feet. It is very likely that if the ground were properly explored, it would be found deeper, but most probably this is as deep as the natives care to dig for it, if they can obtain it elsewhere nearer the surface. It is said to be found in irregular masses, chiefly flat in shape, and from small knobs to pieces weighing several pounds. These are all carefully chopped into small nearly uniform pieces, the object of this being to enable the natives to sell it by measure,—the measures being little "quindas" or open baskets; the natives of the country where it is obtained not only bring it to the coast for barter, but also sell it to the coast natives, who go with goods to purchase it from them.

The blacks of the gum country are so indolent that they will only dig for the gum during and after the last and heaviest rains, about March, April, and May, and these, and June and July, are the months when it almost all makes its appearance, and they will only allow a certain quantity to leave the country, for fear that its price on the coast may fall; hence only a few tons of this beautiful gum are now obtained, where some years ago hundreds were bought. It is said by the natives that no trees grow on or near the places where the gum copal is found, and that even grass grows very sparingly: the very small quantities of red earth and sand sometimes attached to the gum show it to be so highly ferruginous, that I should imagine such was really the case.

The white Angola gum is said to be the product of a tree growing near rivers and water, a little to the interior of the coast. I have never had an opportunity of seeing the tree myself, however.

We now come to one of the most curious products of this interesting country, namely, india-rubber, called by the natives "Tangandando." It had been an article exported in considerable quantities north of the River Congo, and knowing that the plant from which it was obtained grew in abundance in the second region, about sixty miles inland from Ambriz, I distributed a number of pieces of the india-rubber to natives of the interior, and offered a high price for any that might be brought for sale. In a very short time it began to come in, and the quantity has steadily increased to the present day.

The plant that produces it is the giant tree-creeper (*Landolphia, florida?*), covering the highest trees, and growing principally on those near rivers or streams. Its stem is sometimes as thick as a man's thigh, and in the dense woods at Quiballa I have seen a considerable extent of forest festooned down to the ground, from tree to tree, in all directions with its thick stems, like great hawsers; above, the trees were nearly hidden by its large, bright, dark-green leaves, and studded with beautiful bunches of pure white star-like flowers, most sweetly scented. Its fruit is the size of a large orange, of a yellow colour when ripe, and perfectly round, with a hard brittle shell; inside it is full of a soft reddish pulp in which the seeds are contained. This pulp is of a very agreeable acid flavour, and is much liked by the natives. The ripe fruit, when cleaned out, is employed by them to contain small quantities of oil, &c. It is not always easy to obtain ripe seeds, as this creeper is the favourite resort of a villainous, semi-transparent, long legged red ant—with a stinging bite like a red-hot needle—which is very fond of the pulp and seeds.

Every part of this creeper exudes a milky juice when cut or wounded, but unlike the india-rubber tree of America, this milky sap will not run into a vessel placed to receive it, as it dries so quickly as to form a ridge on the wound or cut, which stops its further flow.

The blacks collect it, therefore, by making long cuts in the bark with a knife, and as the milky juice gushes out, it is wiped off continually with their fingers, and smeared on their arms, shoulders, and breast until a thick covering is formed; this is peeled off their bodies and cut into small squares, which are then said to be boiled in water.

From Ambriz the trade in this india-rubber quickly spread south to the River Quanza, from whence considerable quantities are exported.

The ivory that reaches this part of the coast is brought down by natives of the Zombo country. These are similar in appearance to the Mushicongos, to which tribe they are said to be neighbours, and are physically a poor-looking race, dressed mostly in native grass-cloth, and wearing the wool on their heads in very small plaits, thickly plastered with oil and charcoal dust, which they also plentifully apply to their faces and bodies.

They are about thirty days on the journey from their country to the coast, which can therefore be very closely calculated to be about 300 miles distance. The road they follow passes near Bembe, and the caravans shortly afterwards divide into three portions, one taking the road to Moculla, another to Ambrizzette, and the third to Quissembo, the three centres, at present, of the ivory trade. The caravans of ivory generally travel in the "cacimbo" or dry season, on account of the great number of streams and gullies they have to cross on their long journey, and almost impassable in the rainy season. These caravans never bring down any other produce with them but ivory, except at times a few grass-cloths, some bags of white haricot-beans, and fine milk-white onions, neither of which are cultivated by the natives near the coast. The tusks are carried by the natives on their heads or shoulders, and, to prevent their slipping, are fastened in a sort of cage of four short pieces of wood (Plate IV.). Very heavy teeth are slung to a long pole and carried by two blacks. The largest tusks I have seen were two that came to Quissembo, evidently taken from the same animal; they weighed respectively 172 and 174 pounds!

PLATE IV.
1. Ankle-ring—2. Ring to ascend Palm-trees.—3. Cage for carrying Ivory Tusks. 4. Engongui.—5. Fetish figure.—6. Mask.—7. Pillow.

The knives on Plate V. were obtained from natives composing these caravans.

From all the more intelligent natives I always obtained the same information respecting the origin of the ivory brought down to the coast, namely, that it was all from animals killed, and not from elephants found dead. The natives from the interior always laughed at the idea of ivory becoming scarce from the numbers of elephants that must necessarily be killed to supply the large number of tusks annually brought down,—the number slaughtered must therefore be very small in comparison to the living herds they must be in the habit of seeing on the vast plains of the interior. They are said to be shot, and that the natives put such a charge of powder and iron bullets into their guns that when fired from the shoulder the hunter cannot use his gun again that day, so great is the kick he gets from its recoil. I can well understand that this is not an exaggerated account, from the manner in which blacks always load a gun, the charge of powder being one handful, as much as it can hold, then a wadding of baobab fibre, then lead shot, or lead or iron bullets (in default of which they use the heavy round pieces of pisolitic iron ore very common in the country), another wad of baobab fibre, and the gun must then show that it is loaded a "palm," or about eight or nine inches of the barrel.

On festive occasions, or at their burials, the guns are loaded with a tamping of "fuba," or fine mandioca-meal, instead of other wadding, and they then give a terrific report when fired off, and not unfrequently burst.

This coast abounds with fish, but very few of the natives engage in their capture, as they make so much by trading that they will not take the trouble. Several fish, such as the "Pungo," weighing as much as three "arrobas," or ninety-six pounds, visit the coast only in the "cacimbo" or cold season of the year, or from June to August.

The Bay of Musserra is a noted place for large captures of this fine fish, as many as forty or fifty being caught in a day by the natives, with hook and line, from their small curious shaped canoes. It is a very firm-fleshed fish, and cut up, salted, and dried in the sun, was a great article of trade at Musserra, being sold to the natives from the interior, particularly to the "Zombos" composing the caravans of ivory, who are very fond of salt fish. There was a great row in the season 1870, which was a very scarce one for ground-nuts, between the natives of the interior and the blacks at Musserra, on account of the latter taking to collect Adansonia fibre in preference to catching "Pungo," and therefore disappointing the inlanders of their favourite salt delicacy.

The canoes on this part of the coast, and as far north as Cabinda, are very curious, and totally unlike any that I have seen anywhere else. They are composed of two rounded canoes lashed or sewn together below, and open at the top. This aperture is narrow, and each canoe forms, as it were, a long pocket. The natives stand or sit on them with their legs in the canoe, or astride, as most convenient according to the state of the surf, on which these canoes ride beautifully.

The town of Musserra was formerly a large and populous one, but small-pox and "sleep disease" have reduced it to a mere handful.

This "sleep disease" was unknown south of the River Congo, where it formerly attacked the slaves collected in the barracoons for shipment. It suddenly appeared at the town of Musserra alone, where, I was told by the natives, as many as 200 of the inhabitants died of it in a few months. This was in 1870, and, curious to say, it did not spread to the neighbouring towns.

I induced the natives to remove from the old town, and the mortality decreased till the disease died out.

This singular disease appears to be well known at Gaboon, &c., and is said to be an affection of the cerebellum. The subjects attacked by it suffer no pain whatever, but fall into a continual heavy drowsiness or sleep, having to be awakened to be fed, and at last become unable to eat at all, or stand, and die fast asleep as it were. There is no cure known for it, and the patients are said to die generally in about twenty to forty days after being first attacked.

There was nothing in the old town to account for this sudden and singular epidemic; it was beautifully clean, and well built on high, dry ground, surrounded by mandioca plantations, and the last place to all appearance to expect such a curious outbreak.

About four or five miles inland of Musserra, on a ridge of low hills, stands the remarkable granite pillar marked on the charts, and forming a capital landmark to ships at sea (Plate V.).

PLATE V.
Granite Pillar of Musserra.—1. Wooden Trumpet.—2. Hoe.—3. Pipe.—4. Knives.—5 and 6. Clapping Hands, and Answer.

The country at that distance from the coast is singularly wild in appearance, from the whole being broken up into what can only be compared to a vast granite quarry:—huge blocks of this rock, of every imaginable size and shape, are scattered over the hilly ground, thickly interspersed with gigantic baobabs and creepers. Some of the masses of rock imitate grotesquely all manner of objects: a very curious one is exactly like a huge cottage-loaf stuck on the top of a tall slender pillar. Others are generally rounded masses, large and small, piled one on top of another, and poised and balanced in the most fantastic manner. This extraordinary appearance is due to softer horizontal layers or beds in the granite weathering unequally, and to strongly-marked cleavage planes running N.N.E. and S.S.W.

The granite pillar itself stands on the top of one of the last of the low hills forming the rocky ridge that comes down to within a few miles of the coast. It consists of a huge slice or flat piece of granite, facing the sea, standing upright on another block that serves it for a pedestal. The top piece is about forty-five feet high, and twenty-seven broad at the base, and eight to ten feet thick. Its faces correspond to the cleavage plane of the granite of the country, and from large masses that lie around on the same hill, it is clear that these have fallen away from each side, and left it alone standing on the top. The square pedestal on which it stands is about forty feet long, and twenty high, by twenty-seven wide. I climbed once to the top of this square block by the help of a small tree growing against it, and found that the top piece rested on three points that I could just crawl under. Under some lichen growing there I found numbers of a beetle (*Pentalobus barbatus*, Fabr.), which I presented to the British Museum.

A considerable quantity of salt is made by the natives of this part of the coast, from Quissembo to Ambrizzette, particularly at the latter place, in the small salt marshes near the sea, and with which they carry on a trade with the natives from the interior.

At the end of the dry season the women and children divide the surface of these marshes into little square portions or pans, by raising mud walls a few inches high, so as to enclose in each about two or three gallons of the water, saturated with salt from the already nearly evaporated marsh. As the salt crystallizes in the bottom of these little pans, it is taken out, and more water added, and so the process is continued until the marsh is quite dry. In many cases a small channel is cut from the marsh to the sea (generally very close to it) to admit fresh sea-water at high tide.

It is an amusing sight to see numbers of women and children, all stark naked, standing sometimes above their knees in the water, baling it into the "pans" with small open baskets or "quindas," and all singing loudly a monotonous song;—others are engaged in filling large "quindas" with dirty salt from the muddy pans, whilst others again are busily washing the crystallized salt by pouring sea-water over it till all the mud is washed away, and the basketfuls of salt shine in the sun like driven snow.

Towards evening long lines of women and children will be seen carrying to their towns, on their heads, the harvest of salt, and great is the fun and chaff from them if they meet a white man travelling in a hammock,—all laughing and shouting, and wanting to shake hands, and running to keep pace with the hammock-bearers.

The proprietress of each set of little evaporating pans marks them as her property by placing a stick in each corner, to which is attached some "fetish" to keep others from pilfering. This "fetish" is generally a small bundle of strips of cloth or rags, or a small gourd or baobab fruit containing feathers, fowl-dung, "tacula" (red wood), or very often some little clay or wooden figure, grotesquely carved, and coloured red and white.

Quantities of little fish are also captured about the same time from these marshes, being driven into corners, &c., and prevented from returning to the marsh by a mud wall. The water from the enclosure thus formed is then baled out by the women with baskets, and the fish caught in the mud. I have often seen as many as twenty women all standing in a line, baling out the water from a large pool in which they had enclosed shoals of little fish. These are spread out on the ground to dry in the sun, and the stench from them during the process is something terrific. When dry they are principally sold to natives from the interior.

Many kinds of aquatic birds of all sizes flock in the dry season to these marshes, where a rich abundance of finny food awaits them, and it is curious to see what little regard they pay to the women collecting salt or baling water, and singing loudly in chorus, very often quite close to them. The reason of this tameness is that the natives seldom fire at or molest them, only a very few hunters shooting wild-ducks for sale to the white men, though they will always eat any kind of rank gull or other bird that a white man may shoot. Very beautiful are the long lines of spoonbills, flamingoes, and herons of different species, standing peacefully in these shallow marshes, their snow-white plumage and tall graceful forms brightly reflected on the dark unruffled surface of the water.

The marshes on this coast are fortunately not extensive enough to influence much the health of the white residents; they are all perfectly salt, and free from mangrove or other vegetation, and generally dry up completely (with rare exceptions) in the dry season, when sometimes the stench from them is very perceptible.

The worst season for Europeans is about May, June, and July, when the marshes are quite full from the last heavy rains, and exhale no smell whatever.

The point at Musserra is composed of sandstone, the lower beds of which are strongly impregnated with bitumen, so strongly, indeed, that it oozes out in the hot season.

At Kinsao, near Mangue Grande, and a few miles to the interior, a lake of this mineral pitch is said to exist, but of course the natives will not allow a white man to visit the locality to ascertain the fact, and it is also "fetish" for the natives to trade in it. The fear of annexation of the country by the white men has caused the natives to "fetish" and absolutely prohibit even the mention of another very important article—malachite—of which there is every reason to believe a large deposit exists, about six miles up the river at Ambrizzette. The scenery up this little river is very lovely, but the natives will not allow white men to ascend more than a few miles or up to a hill beyond which the deposit or mine of malachite is believed to exist. In the slave-trading time quantities of this mineral in fine lumps used to be purchased of the natives from this locality, but on the occupation of Ambriz by the Portuguese, in 1855, for the purpose of reaching the malachite deposit at Bembe, the natives of Ambrizzette closed the working of their mine, and it remains so to this day, and nothing will induce them to open it again.

I have had many private conversations with them, and tried hard to make them work it again, but, as might be expected, without success.

CHAPTER VI.
AMBRIZ—TRADE—MALACHITE—ROAD TO BEMBE—
TRAVELLING—MOSQUITOES—QUIBALLA TO
QUILUMBO—QUILUMBO TO BEMBE.

Ambriz, seen from the sea, consists of a high rocky cliff or promontory, with a fine bay sweeping with a level beach northward nearly to the next promontory, on which stand the trading factories forming the place called Quissembo, or Kinsembo of the English.

In the bay the little River Loge has its mouth, and marks the northern limit of the Portuguese possession of Angola. The country beyond, described in the last chapter, is in the hands of the natives, under their own laws, and owing no allegiance or obedience to any white power. Ambriz was, up to the year 1855, when it was occupied by the Portuguese, also in the hands of the natives, and was one of the principal ports for the shipment of, and trade in slaves, from the interior.

There were also established there American and Liverpool houses, trading in gum copal, malachite, and ivory, and selling, for hard cash, Manchester and other goods to the slave dealers from Cuba and the Brazils, with which goods the slaves from the interior were all bought by barter from the natives.

The Portuguese, following their usual blind and absurd policy, at once established a custom-house, and levied high duties on all goods imported. The consequence was, that the foreign houses, to escape their exactions, at once removed to Quissembo, on the other side of the River Loge, and the trade of Ambriz was completely annihilated and reduced to zero. For many years the revenue barely sufficed to pay the paltry salaries of the custom-house officials, but when I established myself at Ambriz, I succeeded in inducing the Governor-General of Angola to reduce the duties, so as to enable us at Ambriz to compete successfully with the factories at Quissembo, six miles off, where they paid no duties whatever, with the annual exception of a few pounds' worth of cloth, &c., in "customs" or presents to the natives.

The Governor, Francisco Antonio Gonçalves Cardozo, a naval officer, had the common sense to perceive that moderate duties would yield a greater revenue, and would be the only means of bringing back trade to the place. An import duty of six per cent. ad valorem was decreed, notwithstanding the violent opposition of the petty merchants, and ignorant officials at Loanda. The experiment, it is needless to say, was highly successful, and the receipts of the Ambriz custom-house now amount to a considerable sum, of which a third is devoted to public works. The factories at Quissembo are at present doing but little trade, except in ivory, which has not yet been coaxed back to Ambriz.

The town of Ambriz consists principally of one long, broad street or road, on the ridge that ends at the cliff or promontory forming the southern point of the bay. At the end of the road a small fort has been built, in which are the barracks for the detachment of troops forming the garrison. This useless fort has been a source of considerable profit to the many ill-paid Portuguese governors or commandants of Ambriz, and though it has cost the country thousands of pounds, it is not yet finished. There is a tumble-down house for the commandant, and an attempt at an hospital, also unfinished, though it has been building for many years. There are no quarters for the officers, who live as best they can with the traders, or hire whatever mud or grass huts they can secure.

The custom-house is in ruins, notwithstanding many years of expenditure, for which, in fact, fort, hospital, barracks, custom-house, and all other government and public works might have been built long ago, of stone and building materials from Portugal. A church was commenced to be built by subscriptions, the walls only were raised, and thus it remains to this day. There is a government paid priest who celebrates mass on most Sunday mornings in a small room in the commandant's house, but for whom no school-room, residence, or any convenience whatever is provided, and who lives in a hut in a back street, where he trades for produce with the natives on week days.

The garrison is badly armed and disciplined. Some time ago the soldiers revolted, and for some days amused themselves by firing their muskets about the place, and demanding drink and money from the traders. There was nobody killed or wounded, no house or store robbed or sacked, the mutineers in fact behaving remarkably well. The commandant kept indoors until the news reached Loanda, and after several days the Governor-General arrived in a Portuguese man-of-war with troops, which were disembarked, the valiant Governor-General remaining on board till order was restored, when he landed, had a couple of the ringleaders thrashed, made a speech to the rest of the mutineers, and returned to Loanda, leaving the tall commandant to twirl his moustaches. The Governor-General was at that time an officer called José da Ponte e Horta, and though not one of the most competent men that Portugal has sent to Angola as governor, the inhabitants of Loanda have to thank him for paving a great part of their sandy city.

Were not the natives of Ambriz such a remarkably inoffensive and unwarlike race, they would long ago have driven the Portuguese into the sea. It is a great pity that Portugal should neglect so disgracefully her colonies, so rich in themselves, and offering such wonderful advantages in every way for colonization and development.

In the year 1791 the Portuguese built a fort at Quincollo, about six miles up the River Loge, on a low hill commanding the road from Ambriz to Bembe and St. Salvador, where they then had a large establishment, and the masses of masonry still remain, a standing memorial of the former energy and bravery of the Portuguese who subjugated the then powerful kingdom of Congo and the savage tribes of the coast, so strikingly in contrast to the present spiritless and disgraceful military misrule of Angola.

Ambriz boasts of the only iron pier in Angola, and this was erected at my instigation. It is 200 feet long, and is a great advantage in loading and discharging cargo into or from the lighters.

Ambriz is an open roadstead, and vessels have to anchor at a considerable distance from the beach, and though the surf sometimes interferes with the above operations on the beach, vessels are always safe, such things as storms or heavy seas being unknown.

Behind the beach a salt, marshy plain extends inland for a mile or so, and nearly to Quissembo in a northerly direction. Along the edge of this plain is the road to Quincollo, and many little ravines or valleys lead into it. These, in the hot season particularly, are most lovely in their vegetation, the groups of gigantic euphorbias festooned with many delicate-leaved creepers being especially quaint and beautiful.

A handsome orange and black diurnal moth is found abundantly about Ambriz, and is curious from its exhaling a strong smell of gum benzoin, so strong indeed as to powerfully scent the collecting box. It is the *Eusemia ochracea* of entomologists.

In 1872, the ship "Thomas Mitchell" took a cargo of coals from England to Rio de Janeiro, and after discharging proceeded in ballast to Ambriz. The crew on arrival were suffering from "chigoes" or "jiggers" in their feet, which they contracted in the Brazils. These pests were quickly communicated to the black crews of our boats and introduced on shore, and in a short time every one in Ambriz had them in their feet and hands. Many of the blacks were miserable objects from the ravages of this horrid insect on their feet and legs, in the skin of which they burrow and breed. They gradually extended up the coast, but not towards the interior. By last advices they appear to be dying out at Ambriz. It is to be hoped that such is the case, and that this fresh acquisition to the insect scourges of tropical Africa may be only temporary. A friend just arrived from the coast tells me that they have already reached Gaboon, and they will doubtlessly run all the way up the coast.

Previous to the occupation of Ambriz by the Portuguese in 1855, the natives used to bring down a considerable quantity of fine malachite from Bembe for sale. A Brazilian slave-dealer, a man of great energy and enterprise, called Francisco Antonio Flores, who, after the abolition of the slave-trade, laboured incessantly to develop the resources of Angola, in which effort he sank the large fortune he had previously amassed, obtained the concession of the Bembe mines from the Portuguese Government, who sent an expedition to occupy the country, and succeeded without any opposition on the part of the natives.

In January, 1858, I was engaged by the Western Africa Malachite Copper Mines Company, who had acquired the mines from Senhor Flores, to accompany a party of twelve miners sent under a Cornish mining captain to explore them. We arrived at Bembe on the 8th March, and the next day seven of the men were down with fever; the others also quickly fell ill, and for three months that followed of the heavy rainy season, they passed through great discomforts from want of proper accommodation. Ultimately eight died within the next nine months, and the rest had to be sent home, with the exception of one man and myself. This result was not so much the effect of the climate, as the want of proper lodgings and care.

The superintendent was at that time the Portuguese commandant, who of course did not interfere with the mining captain, an ignorant man, who made the men work in the same manner of day and night shifts as if they were in Cornwall, in the full blaze of the sun, in their wet clothes, &c.

An English superintendent next arrived, but he unfortunately was addicted to intemperance, and soon died from the effects of the brandy bottle. After being at Bembe eight or nine months, the mining captain, either from stupidity or wilfulness, not only had not discovered a single pound of malachite, but insisted that there was none in the place, where the natives for years previously had extracted from 200 to 300 tons every dry season! In view of his conduct I took upon myself the responsibility of taking charge of the mining operations, and sent him back to England. A few days after we discovered fine blocks of malachite, fifteen tons of which I sent to the Company in the same steamer that took him home.

It would not interest the reader to describe minutely the causes that led gradually to the abandonment of the working of these mines, and to the heavy loss sustained by the Company, but I am convinced that, had duly qualified and experienced men directed the working from the beginning, they would have proved a success. Many hundred tons of malachite were afterwards raised, with the help of a very few white miners, but too late to correct the previous mistakes and losses.

During the years 1858 and 1859 I travelled the road from Ambriz to Bembe eight times, and in the month of April 1873, I went again, for the last time, with my wife.

Lieutenant Grandy and his brother had been our guests at Ambriz, where we had supplied them with the greater part of the beads and goods they required for their arduous journey into the interior. These gentlemen, it will be recollected, were sent by the Royal Geographical Society to discover the source of the Congo, and to meet and aid Dr. Livingstone in the interior should he have crossed the continent from the east coast, as it was imagined he might probably do.

We had arranged to proceed together from Ambriz as far as Bembe, but owing to the great mortality in the country from two successive visitations of small-pox, which had ravaged the coast, we were unable to obtain the necessary number of carriers. The two brothers alone required nearly 200, and as only a few comparatively could be had at a time, they went singly first, and, about a week after they had both started, my wife and myself were able to get together sufficient carriers to leave also.

To travel in a country like Angola it is necessary to be provided with almost everything in the way of food and clothing, and goods for money, and as everything has to be carried on men's heads, a great number of carriers are necessarily requisite.

The "tipoia," or hammock, is the universal travelling apparatus in Angola (Plate I.), and is of two forms, the simple hammock slung to a palm pole (the stem of the leaf of a *Metroxylon*, Welw.), which is very strong and extremely light, or the same with a light-painted waterproof cover, and curtains, very comfortable to travel in, and always used by the Portuguese to the interior of Loanda, where the country is more open, and better paths or roads exist, but they would quickly be torn to pieces north, and on the road to Bembe, from the very dense bush, and in the wet season the very high grass; consequently the plain hammock and pole only are generally employed, the traveller shading himself from the sun by a movable cover held in position by two cords, or by using a white umbrella. When travelling long distances six or eight bearers are necessary: the two hammock-carriers generally run at a trot for about two hours at a stretch, when another couple take their places.

On any well-known road the natives have established changing or resting places, which, when not at a town, are generally at some shady tree or place where water is to be had,—or at the spots where fairs are held, or food cooked and exposed for sale by the women.

When the road was clear of grass, in the dry season, I have more than once travelled from Ambriz to Bembe—a distance of not less than 130 miles—in four days, with only eight bearers and light luggage, and this without in any way knocking up or distressing the carriers, and only running from daybreak to nightfall;—very often they joined in a "batuco" or dance, for several hours into the night, at the town I slept at, and were quite fresh and ready to start next morning.

It is only the stronger blacks that are good hammock-bearers, especially the coast races, very few of the natives of the interior, such as the Mushicongos, being sufficiently powerful to carry a hammock for any distance. The motion is extremely disagreeable at first, from the strong up and down jerking experienced, but one soon becomes quite used to it, and falls asleep whilst going at full trot, just as if it were perfectly still. The natives of Loanda and Benguella, though not generally such strong carriers as the Ambriz blacks, take the hammock at a fast walk instead of the sharp trot of the latter, and consequently hammock travelling there is very lazy and luxurious.

The pole is carried on the shoulder, and rests on a small cushion generally made of fine grass-cloth stuffed with wild cotton, the silky fibre in the seed-pod of the "Mafumeira," or cotton-wood tree (*Eriodendron anfractuosum*), or "isca," a brown, woolly-like down covering the stems of palm-trees. Each bearer carries a forked stick on which to rest the pole when changing shoulders, and also to ease the load by sticking the end of it under the pole behind their backs, and stretching out their arm on it. No one who has not tried can form an idea what hard, wearying work it is to carry a person in a hammock, and it is wonderful how these blacks will run with one all day, in the hot sun, nearly naked, with bare shaved heads, and not feel distressed.

On arriving at any stream or pool they dash at once into the water, and wash off the perspiration that streams from their bodies, and I never heard of any ill consequence occurring from this practice. The hammock-bearers do not as a rule carry loads; by native custom they are only obliged to carry the white man's bed, his provision-box, and one portmanteau. To take my wife, myself, a tent—as it was the rainy season—provisions, bedding, and a few changes of clothes, only what was absolutely necessary for a month's journey, we had to engage exactly thirty carriers: this included our cook and his boy with the necessary pots and pans; our "Jack Wash," as the laundry-boys are called, with his soap and irons; and one man with the drying-papers and boxes for collecting plants and insects. We also took a Madeira cane chair, very useful to be carried in across the streams or marshes we should meet with.

All being ready we started off, passing Quincollo and arriving at Quingombe, where we encamped for the night on top of a hill, to be out of the way, as I thought, of a peculiarly voracious mosquito very abundant there, and of which I had had experience in my former journeys to and from Bembe.

I shall never forget the first night I passed there in going up to the mines with the twelve miners. There was at that time a large empty barracoon built of sticks and grass for the accommodation of travellers. Soon after sunset a hum like that of distant bees was heard, and a white mist seemed to rise out of the marshy land below, which was nothing less than a cloud of mosquitoes. The men were unprovided with mosquito nets, and the consequence was that sleep was perfectly out of the question, so they sat round the table smoking and drinking coffee, and killing mosquitoes on their hands and faces all night long. I had been given an excellent mosquito bar or curtain, but the ground was so full of sand-fleas, that although I was not troubled with mosquitoes, the former kept me awake and feverish. In the morning we laughed at our haggard appearance, and swollen faces and hands; luckily we were not so troubled any more on our journey up.

Where mosquitoes are in such abundance, nothing but a proper curtain will avail against them; smoking them out is of very little use, as only such a large amount of acrid smoke will effectually drive them away as to make the remedy almost unbearable. The substances usually burnt in such cases are dry cow-dung, mandioca-meal, or white Angola gum.

There are several species of mosquito in Angola; that found in marshes is the largest, and is light brown in colour, and very sluggish in its flight or movements. When the fellow settles to insert his proboscis, it is quite sufficient to put the tip of a finger on him to annihilate him, but none of the others can be so easily killed; two or three species—notably a little black shiny fellow, only found near running water—are almost impossible to catch when settled and sucking, even with the most swiftly delivered slap. Another species is beautifully striped or banded with black, body and legs.

Mosquitoes rarely attack in the daytime, except in shady places, where they are fond of lying on the under side of leaves of trees. Some with large beautiful plumed antennæ appear at certain times of the year in great numbers, and are said to be the males, and are not known to bite or molest in any way.

Although we pitched our tent on top of a hill to escape the marsh mosquitoes, and had a terrific rain-storm nearly the whole of the night, they found us out, and in the morning the inner side of our tent was completely covered with them;—had we not slept under a good mosquito net, we should have passed just such another night as I have described. We had to stop a second night on this hill to wait for our full number of carriers. The scenery from it is magnificent, low hills covered with dense bush of the prickly acacia tree (*A. Welwitschii*), high grass, baobabs and euphorbias, and in the low places a great abundance of a large aloe, with pale crimson flowers in tall spikes.

At last all loads were properly distributed and secured in the "mutetes," an arrangement in which loads are very conveniently carried. They are generally made from the palm leaves, the leaflets of which are woven into a kind of basket, leaving the stems only about five or six feet long; a little shoe or slipper, made of wood or hide, is secured to the under side. When the carrier wishes to rest, he bends down his head until the palm stems touch the ground, and the load is then leant up against a tree. If there is not a tree handy, then the end of their stick or staff being inserted into the shoe, forms with the two ends three legs, on which it stands securely. This shoe is also useful with the staff when on the journey, to rest the carrier for a few minutes by easing the weight of the load off his head without setting it down. The natives of the interior carry loads on their heads that they are unable to lift easily from the ground, and the "mutete" is therefore very convenient. In carrying a large bag of produce, a long stick is tied on to each side, to act in the same way as the "mutete."

In four days we arrived at Quiballa, where we rested a couple of days, to collect plants and some fine butterflies from the thick surrounding woods, and to dry the plants we had gathered thus far. The country we had passed was comparatively level, and the scenery for the most part was very like that of a deserted park overgrown with rank grass and weeds.

As Quiballa is approached the country becomes very hilly in all directions, and the vegetation changes to fine trees and creepers, conspicuous amongst which is the india-rubber plant already described.

Quiballa is a large town most picturesquely situated on a low, flat-topped hill, surrounded on all sides by other higher hills, and separated from them by a deep ravine filled with magnificent forest vegetation, and in the bottom of which a shallow stream of the clearest water runs swiftly over its fantastic rocky bed—all little waterfalls and shady transparent pools. Our finest specimens of butterflies, such as *Godartia Trajanus, Romaleosoma losinga, R. medon, Euryphene Plistonax* and others, were collected in these lovely woods; they do not come out into the sunny open, but flit about in the shadiest part under the trees, flying near the ground, and occasionally settling on a leaf or branch on which a streak of sunshine falls through the leafy vault above. Other species, such as the Papilios (*P. menestheus, P. brutus, P. demoleus, P. erinus, Diadema misuppus*), &c. &c., on the contrary, we only found in the full sunshine, on the low bushes and flowering plants, skirting, as with a broad belt, the woods or forest.

The change in vegetation from the coast to Quiballa may be due not only to difference of altitude, but partly to the rock of the country, which is a large-grained, very quartzose mica rock or gneiss from the coast to near Quiballa, where it changes to a soft mica slate, easily decomposed by water and atmospheric influences. Several species of birds, very abundant on the coast and as far as Matuta, disappear about Quiballa, the most notable being the common African crow (*Corvus scapulatus*), the brilliantly-coloured starlings (*Lamprocolius*), and the several rollers; doves also, so abundant on the coast, are comparatively rare after passing Quiballa.

The *Coracias caudata*, the most beautiful of the African rollers, has a very extraordinary manner of flying, tumbling about in a zig-zag fashion in the air as if drunk, and chattering loudly all the time. I once shot at one on the top of a high tree at Matuta; it fell dead, as I thought, but on picking it up I was gladly surprised to find it quite uninjured, and only stunned apparently. I placed it in a hastily-constructed cage, and took it with me to Bembe, where it became quite tame, and I had it several months, till my boy, feeding it one morning, left the door of its cage open, and it flew away. In its native state it feeds principally on grasshoppers; in captivity its food was mostly raw meat, which it ate greedily.

The starlings of darkest shades of blue, with bright yellow eyes, are strikingly beautiful when seen flying, the sunshine reflecting the metallic lustre of their plumage.

The cooing of the doves serves the natives at night instead of a clock, as they coo at the same hours as the common cock, and in travelling, if the natives are asked the time during the night, they always refer to the "dove having sung," as they term it, or not. Its cooing a little before day-dawn is the signal to prepare for the start that day.

At the town of Quirillo, where we slept one night, the Madeira chair first came into use, to cross a stream and marsh in which the water came up to the men's necks. Our hammock-boys thought it fine fun to pass us over the different streams in the chair; all twelve would stand in the water close together, with the chair on their shoulders, and pass my wife across first, singing in chorus, "Mundelle mata-bicho, Mundelle mata-bicho" (Mundelle = white-man, mata-bicho = a "dash" of a drink of rum). On landing her safely they would yell and whistle like demons, accompanied by all the rest on the banks, and splash and dabble about like ducks in the water. The chair would then come back for me, and the same scene be again enacted. A bottle of rum, or a couple of bunches of beads, was always the reward for crossing us over without wetting us.

Quiballa is by far the largest town to be met with from Ambriz, and contains several hundred huts distributed irregularly over the flat top of the hill on which it stands. The huts are square, built of sticks covered with clay, and roofed with grass. The principal room in the largest hut was swept out, and placed at our disposal by the king, and we made ourselves very comfortable in it. The king, Dom Paolo, is a fine, tall old negro, and knowing of our arrival sent his son and a number of men to meet us, when they took my wife's hammock, and raced her into the town at a great pace. He has considerable influence in the country, where his is an important town, as it marks the limits of the coast or Ambriz race, and that of the Mushicongo tribe beyond.

There is a good deal of rivalry between the two races;—the Ambriz blacks do not like going beyond Quiballa, and the Mushicongos object to go into the Ambriz country. Before the road was taken possession of by the Portuguese, Quiballa was the great halting-place for the two tribes, the Mushicongos bringing the proceeds of the copper mines at Bembe to sell to the Ambriz natives, who then carried it to the traders on the coast. With the increased trade in other produce, a great deal of this separation has been done away with, and both tribes now mingle more freely; but at the time I was engaged at the Bembe mines we were obliged to have a large store at Quiballa to receive loads going up from Ambriz, and copper ore coming down from Bembe, and there change carriers.

The Ambriz negroes, being very much stronger, never objected to any loads, however heavy, some of these going up the country with sixteen or twenty carriers, such as the heavy pieces of the steam-engine, saw-mill, pumps, &c. There was great difficulty in inducing the Mushicongos to take these heavy and very often cumbersome loads from Quiballa to Bembe, and once, when loads for upwards of 1000 carriers had accumulated at the store, I was obliged to hit upon the following plan to get the Mushicongos to take them up, and it succeeded admirably.

I engaged 1000 carriers at Bembe to go empty-handed to Quiballa for the cargo there, and paid them only the customary number of beads for rations on the road, rations for the return journey to be paid at Quiballa, and pay for the whole journey at Bembe, on delivery of the loads. My calculation was that the greater number would be forced from hunger to take them, and so it happened. The morning after we arrived at Quiballa they all flatly refused to take a single load of the machinery in the store;—I very quietly told them they might go about their business, and for three days I was yelled at by them, but they were at last forced to accept my terms, and I returned to Bembe with 800 loads.

It was at Quiballa that we were so fortunate as to obtain specimens of the flowers, and a quantity of ripe seeds of the beautiful plant named *Camoensia maxima* by its discoverer, Dr. Welwitsch. We saw it growing along the sides of the road as soon as we left the gneiss formation and entered on the mica slate, but most abundantly in the more bare places on the sides of the hills at Quiballa, in the very hard clay of the decomposed mica slate.

PLATE VI.
VIEW IN THE HILLY COUNTRY OF QUIBALLA—CAMOENSIA
MAXIMA.

The *Camoensia maxima* (Plate VI.) grows as a hard, woody bush, with rather straggling long branches covered with fine large leaves, and bearing bunches of flowers, the lower, and by far the largest petal of which is shaped like a shell, of a delicate creamy white, with its edges exquisitely crisped, bordered with a golden rim, and nearly the size of an open hand. Its roots spread underground to great distances and shoot out into other plants, so that on attempting to remove what we thought nice small plants, we always came on great thick roots which we followed and found to proceed from old bushes at a considerable distance. Several small plants that we brought away alive died subsequently at Ambriz. Half a dozen of the seeds germinated on arrival at Kew Gardens, so that I hope this lovely flower will be shortly in cultivation, a welcome addition to our hot-houses. All the plants that we collected and dried are deposited in the herbarium at Kew Gardens.

A peculiarity of the towns on the coast inhabited by the Ambriz blacks, and which disappears inland, is their being surrounded by a thick, high belt or hedge of a curious, thin, very branching Euphorbia.

The huts in coast towns are all built separately, but near one another, in a clear space, and not separated by trees or hedges; in the interior, however, the space occupied by the towns is very much larger, and many of the huts are built in a square piece of ground and enclosed by a hedge either of a square-stemmed, prickly, cactus-like euphorbia, or more generally of the Physic-nut plant (*Jatropha curcas*), the "Purgueira" of the Portuguese, and from the greater number of trees and palms left standing, the towns are very much prettier, some being remarkably picturesque. Most of them are situated in woods, which are not found in the littoral region. The huts of the Mushicongos, from the greater abundance of building materials, are very much larger than those of the Ambriz blacks, and very often contain two rooms. The towns of both are remarkably clean, and are always kept well swept, as are also the interiors of their huts;—their brooms are a bundle of twigs, and the dust, ashes, &c., are always thrown into the bush surrounding the towns.

A cleanly habit of all blacks, and one which it always struck me might be imitated with advantage by more civilized countries, is that of always turning away their faces to expectorate, and invariably covering it with dust or sand with their feet.

At certain places on the road, generally in the vicinity of water, or where several trees afford a convenient shade, a kind of little market is held all day, of plantains, green indian-corn, mandioca roots, and other articles of food for the supply of the carriers or natives passing up and down. Here the women from the neighbouring towns come with their pots, and cook food, such as dry fish and beans, and sell "garapa" or "uallua," as a kind of beer made from indian-corn is called.

My wife, of course, excited the greatest curiosity in all the towns we passed through; only two white women (both Portuguese) had before made the journey to Bembe, and the remarks and observations made on her appearance, principally by the women, were often very amusing. One old woman at a town where we stayed to breakfast, and who was the king's mother, after watching us for some time, expressed her satisfaction at our conduct, and said we appeared to be a very loving pair, as I had helped my wife first to food and drink. She was very thankful for a cup of coffee, and a handful of lumps of sugar for her cough. Their greatest astonishment, however, was at our india-rubber bed and bath, and the whole town would flock round in breathless amazement to see them blown out ready for use, when our tent had been put up. Some would ask to be allowed to touch them, and would then look quite frightened at their peculiar feel.

In the mornings on coming out of our tent we would generally find a large audience squatted on the ground waiting for our appearance, to wish us good morning, though curiosity to see the finishing touches of our toilette was the principal cause.

My wife's last operations of hair-dressing, which could not be conveniently effected in the closed tent, seemed to cause them most surprise. Beyond this very natural curiosity to see us, we were never once annoyed by any rudeness or impropriety on the part of the natives.

Having rested a couple of days at Quiballa, we again started on our journey. The road (which is nowhere other than a narrow path, only admitting the passage of blacks in single file), after leaving Quiballa, winds around some rocky hills, which are succeeded by a couple of miles of level valley thickly grown with cane and very high grass, until the hill called Tuco is reached, the first great sudden elevation. On the left is a deep valley, filled with an almost impenetrable forest of the most luxuriant foliage and creepers; the great trunks and branches of the high trees are mostly white and shiny, and contrast in a singular manner with the dark green of their leaves. On the right the hill-side is also covered with trees and bush on which was growing abundantly a beautiful creeper, bearing large handsome leaves and bright yellow flowers (*Luffa sp.*). From the top, looking back towards Quiballa, a magnificent view is obtained. As far as the eye can reach is seen a succession of forest-covered mountains brightly lit in the cloudless sun to the distant horizon, shaded off into a haze of lovely blue. It is almost impossible to imagine a more exquisite panorama, and words fail to describe its beauty and grandeur.

After this hill is passed, the country continues comparatively level for some miles, and is very beautiful, being covered with dense vegetation, in which are seen abundance of dark feathery palms, relieved by the bright green patches of the banana groves, planted round the little towns. The soil is very fertile, and many ground-nut and mandioca plantations are seen everywhere.

Our first halt was at Ngungungo, a large and very picturesque town, where there is a considerable trade carried on in mandioca root and its different preparations, as well as in beans and ground-nuts, the produce of the country around.

After passing this town the road becomes very rocky and stony, necessitating getting out of the hammocks and walking a good deal over the rough ground. Farther on, another steep but bare hill had to be ascended, and finally we reached a little new town called Quioanquilla, where we slept. This had been a large and important town, but the natives having robbed several caravans going up to the mines, the Portuguese punished them by burning it some years ago. We saw a considerable quantity of wild pineapples growing about this town, but the natives make no use of its fine fibre, contenting themselves with eating the unripe fruit.

Next day's journey brought us, early in the afternoon, to a very prettily situated new town, of which a little old woman was the queen; her two sons were the head men, and we were most hospitably received by them.

We had, fortunately, thus far escaped rain-storms during the day whilst travelling; rain had always come down at night, when we were comfortably housed in our tent or in the hut at Quiballa. We put up our tent in an open space in the middle of the town, and took the precaution, as usual, of cutting a small trench round it to carry away the water in case of rain. When we retired the weather was fine, but we had not been asleep long before we were awakened by a terrific thunderstorm, accompanied by torrents of rain. The trench overflowed, and a stream of water began to enter our tent. In the greatest hurry I cut another trench along the side of our bed, a foot wide and about nine inches deep, and for two hours did this drain run full of water, such was the downpour of rain. Next morning we continued our journey, and in about half-an-hour's time arrived at a rivulet that drained what was usually a large marsh, but the storm of the previous night had turned the marsh into a lake and the rivulet into a roaring stream quite impassable. After trying it lower down, and finding we could not ford it, we had no alternative but to return to the town and remain there for that day, or till the water should have subsided sufficiently to enable us to cross. The remainder of the day we employed in collecting insects and in drying the plants we had gathered the last few days.

A child was born whilst we were in this town, and, being a girl, it was at once named Rose, after my wife, who had therefore to make the mother a present of a piece of handkerchiefs and an extra fine red cotton one for the baby.

Next day we were able to pass the swollen stream in our chair, after a couple of hours spent in cutting away branches of trees, &c., that obstructed the passage, at a place where the depth of water was about five feet. In a fish-trap I here found the curious new fish described by Dr. A. Günther, and named by him *Gymnallabes apus* ('Annals and Magazine of Natural History' for August, 1873).

PLATE VII.
QUILUMBO.

That day's journey, through a country alternately covered with lovely forest and high grass, brought us to the large town of Quilumbo, beautifully situated in a forest, and with a great number of oil-palm trees (Plate VII.). This is at present the largest and most important town on the road to Bembe, containing several hundred huts and quite a swarm of inhabitants. About noon we halted for breakfast at a market-place near a town on the River Lifua. Here were about forty or fifty armed blacks, with the king from the neighbouring town, all getting rapidly drunk on "garapa," or indian-corn beer; their faces and bodies painted bright red, with a few white spots, looking like so many stage demons, dancing, singing, and flourishing their guns about. They were all going to a town where we heard the kings of five towns were to have their heads cut off that day for complicity in the murder of a woman by one of them. They were accompanied by a man blowing a large wooden trumpet of most extraordinary form (Plate V.).

This trumpet is made of the hollow root and stem of a tree, said to grow in the mud of rivers and marshes; it does not appear to have been thinned away much at its narrow end, but seems to have grown naturally from the large flat root to a thin stem at a short distance above it. I immediately wanted to buy this instrument, but nothing would induce the king to part with it till I offered to exchange it for a brass bugle. I had to give them a "mucanda" or order for one at our store at Ambriz; even then it was not delivered to me, but the king agreed to send one of his sons to Ambriz with it on my return from Bembe, which he did, and thus I became possessed of it.

Next day's journey was through pretty undulating country, covered principally with high grass, and after passing a couple of small towns we arrived, early in the afternoon, at the River Luqueia, which we passed over on a very good plank bridge, just built by the Portuguese officer commanding the small detachment at Bembe. Here our carriers stopped for about an hour, bathing in the river, and dressing themselves in their best cloths and caps, that they had brought with them carefully packed—so as to make their appearance in a dandy condition on entering Bembe, which we did in about half-an-hour's time, having to walk up a stiff hill, too steep to be carried up in our hammocks.

We had thus travelled the whole distance from Ambriz to Bembe, which, as I have before stated, is certainly not less than 130 miles, in eight travelling days. This will give some idea of the endurance of the Ambriz natives, as, from having to take down and pack the tent every morning, and make hot tea or coffee before starting, it was never before seven or eight o'clock that we were on the move. Moreover, from the rain and heavy dew at night, the high grass was excessively wet, and it would not do to start till it had somewhat dried in the morning sun. In going through woods we generally got out of our hammocks in the grateful, cool shade, and collected butterflies, the finest being found in such places. In rocky and hilly places my wife, of course, could not get over the ground on foot so quickly as a man might have done.

A description of the dress she adopted may be useful to other ladies who may travel in similar wild countries, as she found it exceedingly comfortable and convenient for going through wet grass and tangled bush, and through the excessively spiny trees and thorny bushes of the first thirty or forty miles of the road. It was very simple and loose, and consisted of one of my coloured cotton shirts instead of the usual dress-body, and the skirt made short and of a strong material, fastening the shirt round the waist; either or both could then be easily and promptly changed as required.

PLATE VIII.
BEMBE VALLEY.

CHAPTER VII.
BEMBE—MALACHITE DEPOSIT—ROOT PARASITE—
ENGONGUI—MORTALITY OF CATTLE—FAIRS—KING OF
CONGO—RECEPTIONS—CUSTOMS—SAN SALVADOR—
FEVERS—RETURN TO AMBRIZ.

Bembe is the third great elevation, and it stands boldly and cliff-like out of the broad plain on which we have been travelling, and at its base runs the little river Luqueia.

Approaching it from the westward, we see a high mountain to the right of the plateau of Bembe, separated from it by a narrow gorge thickly wooded that drains the valley, separating in its turn the table-land of Bembe from the high flat country beyond, in a north and easterly direction. This valley, in which the great deposit of malachite exists, is about a mile long in a straight line and runs N.N.W. by S.S.E. (Plate VIII.).

It is a *cul-de-sac* at its northern end, terminating in a beautiful waterfall which the waters of a rivulet have worn in the clay slate of the country. This rivulet, after running at the bottom of the valley, takes a sudden bend at its southern end, and escapes through the narrow gorge described above as separating the peak or mountain from the table-land of Bembe. The side of the valley next to Bembe is very steep along its whole length, and shows the clay slate of the country perfectly; the other side, however, is a gradual slope, and is covered by a thick deposit of clayey earths, in which the malachite is irregularly distributed for the whole length of the valley.

The malachite is often found in large solid blocks;—one resting on two smaller ones weighed together a little over three tons, but it occurs mostly in flat veins without any definite dip or order, swelling sometimes to upwards of two feet in thickness, and much fissured in character from admixture with dark oxide of iron, with which it is often cemented to the clay in which it is contained.

Two kinds of clay are found, a ferruginous red, and an unctuous black variety. The malachite occurs almost entirely in the former. A large proportion was obtained in the form of small irregularly-shaped shot, by washing the clay in suitable apparatus. Large quantities had been raised by the natives from this valley before the country was taken possession of by the Portuguese.

For about fifteen years previously, as before stated, from 200 to 300 tons per annum had been brought down to Ambriz by the natives for sale. The mining captain sent out by the English Company did not judiciously employ his force of miners in properly exploring the deposit, so that its extent was never fully ascertained; no shafts were sunk to more than six or eight fathoms in depth at the bottom of the valley, from the quantity of water met with, but in several places the bottom of these shafts was found to be pure solid malachite. In no case was malachite ever found in the clay-slate rock of the country, and there can be no doubt that this vast deposit was brought and deposited in the valley by the agency of water. No other mineral is to be found in the valley, and only some rounded, water-worn pieces of limestone were found in the clay and associated with the malachite.

In some pieces of this a few crystals of atacamite are to be rarely seen. The clay-slate is completely bare of minerals,—with very few veins of quartz, which is highly crystalline,—has well-defined cleavage planes, with a strike of N.W. by S.E., and dips to the S.S.W. at an angle of about 55°.

In no part of Angola, except at Mossamedes, have any regular lodes or deposits of copper or other metals (except iron) been found *in situ*; all bear unmistakable evidences of having been brought from elsewhere, and deposited by the action of water in the places where they are now found.

I have no doubt that the country farther to the interior will be found immensely rich—in copper principally—where the lodes most likely exist that have supplied the enormous amount of copper carbonates found all over Angola, and farther north at Loango.

Some idea may be formed of the great extent of the Bembe deposit, if we consider the manner in which the natives formerly extracted the malachite. It was entirely by means of little round pits, about three or four feet in diameter, sunk in the bottom of the valley and along its whole length, particularly at several places where the water draining from the country above had washed away the clay, and formed little openings on the same level as the bottom of the valley. When I arrived at Bembe, many of these pits were still open for a couple of fathoms deep, as many as eight or nine pits being sunk together in a rich spot. They sunk them only in the dry season, and as deep as four or five fathoms, but of course they were never carried down quite perpendicularly, but in an irregular zigzag fashion, and not being timbered they often fell together, and numbers of blacks were buried alive in them every year. We several times came across bones of blacks who had thus lost their lives. During the rainy season, of course, these pits were filled up with water and mud, and fresh ones had to be dug in the succeeding dry season.

To ascend and descend them the natives drove wooden pegs into the walls, and their only mining tools were the little hoes used in clearing and cultivating the ground, and the cheap spear-pointed knives, ten or eleven inches long, they received in barter at Ambriz from the traders.

The mines belonged to several of the towns in the immediate neighbourhood, principally to one called Matuta; but they allowed the natives of other towns to extract malachite from them, on payment of a certain quantity of the ore they raised.

The natives of Ambriz who went up to Bembe to buy malachite of the Mushicongos were seldom allowed to pass the River Luqueia, where the malachite was brought down for sale by measure, in little baskets, being like the red gum copal, broken into moderate-sized pieces, except the finer lumps, which were sold entire. Most of the malachite has since been obtained by means of levels driven into the side from the bottom of the valley, but the great mass, below the level at which water is reached, remains practically untouched.

The failure of the English Company, from causes to which it is here unnecessary further to advert, caused the works at the mines to be gradually abandoned, and for the last few years the Portuguese have allowed the blacks to work them in their own fashion again; and I was very sorry to see the place in a complete state of ruin, with only a few stone walls overgrown with a luxuriant growth of creepers and other plants to mark the places where the houses and stores formerly stood, and where several hundred natives used to be daily at work.

During the years 1858 and 1859, when I was first at Bembe, any number of natives could be had from the neighbouring towns, willing to work at the mines, and as many as 200 to 300 were daily employed, principally in carrying the ore and clay to the washing-floors, cutting timber, clearing bush, &c.; they were generally engaged for a week's time, their pay ranging from one to three cotton handkerchiefs, and twenty or thirty beads for rations per day. Some few worked steadily for several weeks or even months, when they would go off to their towns, with perhaps only a few handkerchiefs, leaving the rest of their earnings to the care of some friend at Bembe till their return, as, if they took such an amount of wealth to their towns, they ran the risk of being accused of "fetish" and of having the whole taken from them, with perhaps a beating besides. Very often they would go "on the spree" for a week or more till they had spent it all on drink and rioting, when they would return to visit their towns nearly as poor as when they arrived.

Our best workmen were the soldiers of the garrison, mostly blacks and mulattoes from Loanda, and belonging to a sapper corps, and consequently having some knowledge of working, and of tools and implements. It was great trouble to teach the natives the use of the pick and shovel, and the wheelbarrow was a special difficulty and stumbling-block;—when not carrying it on their heads, which they always did when it was empty, two or three would carry it; but the most amusing manner in which I saw it used, was once where a black was holding up the handles, but not pushing at all, whilst another in front was walking backward, and turning the wheel round towards him with his hands. As many as 1000 carriers at a time could easily be had from the neighbouring towns to carry the copper ore to Quiballa or Ambriz, by giving them two or three days' notice.

The carriers, either at Bembe or on the coast, are always accompanied by a head-man, called a "Capata" (generally from each town, and bringing from 10 to 100 or more carriers), who is responsible for the loads and men. The load of the carriers used to be two and a half "arrobas" or eighty pounds of malachite, and some few strong fellows used to carry two such loads on their heads all the way to Ambriz. Their pay was one piece of ten cotton handkerchiefs, and 300 blue glass beads for each journey—the "Capata" taking double pay and no load. This was equal to about 5*l.* per ton carriage to Ambriz. At present the cost would be much more on account of the great decrease of population from several epidemics of small-pox, and from the very large carrying trade in ground-nuts and coffee.

At the end of the valley, where it joins the narrow gorge that drains it, an enormous mass of a very hard metamorphic limestone, destitute of fossil remains, rises from the bottom to a height of about thirty feet, and in it are contained two caverns or large chambers. This mass of rock is imbedded in a dense forest, and is overgrown by trees and enormous creepers, the stems of which, like great twisted cables, hang down through the crevices and openings to the ground below.

Great numbers of bats inhabit the roof of the darkest of these caverns, and some that I once shot were greatly infested with a large, and very active, nearly white species of the curious spider-looking parasite Nyctiribia, that lives on this class of animals.

In the thick damp shade of the trees surrounding this mass of rock, we collected the rose-coloured flowers of that extremely curious root parasite, the *Thonningea sanguinea* (Dr. Hooker, 'Transactions of the Linnean Society,' 1856).—These specimens are now in the Kew Museum.

The Portuguese built a fine little fort at Bembe, with a dry ditch round it, which has stood one or two sieges; but the Mushicongos are a cowardly set without any idea of fighting, so that they were easily beaten off by the small garrison.

At the time of my first arrival at Bembe, there were about 200 men in garrison, who were well shod, clothed, and cared for. They had a band of music of some fifteen performers, and the manner in which it was got up was most amusing. One of the officers sent to Loanda for a number of musical instruments, and picking out a man for each, he was given the option of becoming a musician, or of being locked up in the calaboose on bread and water for a certain period. They all, of course, preferred the former alternative, and there happening to be a mulatto in the garrison who had been a bandsman, he was elevated to the post of bandmaster, and forthwith ordered to teach the rest.

The performances of this band may be best left to the imagination, but wonderful to relate, the governor (Andrade) used to take pleasure in listening to the excruciating din, which would have delighted a Hottentot, and would make them play under his quarters several evenings a week.

On the anniversary of the signing of the "Carta Constitucional," a great day in Portugal, the same governor invited us all to a picnic at the top of the Peak, where a large tent had been erected and a capital breakfast provided: a three-pounder gun had been dragged up to fire salutes, and we enjoyed a very pleasant day. From the summit a magnificent view of the surrounding country is obtained, and on descending, we proceeded to visit the town of Matuta, some little distance off. On approaching the town, the band struck up, accompanied by the big drum beaten to the utmost. Our approach had not been perceived, and at the unaccountable uproar of the band as we entered the town, a most laughable effect was produced on the inhabitants, who fled in all directions in the greatest dismay, with the children crying and yelling as only small negroes can. After our sitting down, and holding out bottles of rum and bunches of beads, they quickly became convinced of our peaceable intentions and flocked round us, and in a little time the king, a short thin old man, made his appearance, dressed in a long red cloak, a large cavalry helmet on his head, and carrying a cutlass upright in his hand, at arm's-length. After the usual drinks and compliments, the band played again, to the now intense enjoyment of the inhabitants, who capered and danced and shouted around like demons. So great was the effect and pleasure produced on them by the band, that they made a subscription of beads, and presented it to the performers.

From this town we went to another close by, separated only by a small stream, which was governed by another king, also a very old man, who, we found, was nearly dying of age and rheumatism. In crossing the stream, our king of the red cloak and helmet presented a comical appearance, for to save his finery from wetting, he tucked it up rather higher than was necessary or dignified. This same king, having on one occasion brought into Bembe a couple of blacks who had robbed their loads in coming up the country from Ambriz, got so drunk upon the rum which he received as part of the reward for capturing them, that his attendants stripped him of his state uniform and helmet, and left him by the side of the road stark naked, with a boy sitting by his side holding an umbrella over him till his everyday clothes were sent from his town, and he was sufficiently sober to walk home. In Africa, as everywhere else, there is often but a step from the sublime to the ridiculous!

Mr. Flores's agent at Bembe used to buy ivory, though after a time he had to give up trading there, partly on account of having to carry up the goods for barter from Ambriz, and from the natives wanting as much for the tusks as they were in the habit of getting on the coast;—blacks having no regard whatever for time or distance, eight or ten days' journey more or less being to them perfectly immaterial. The road followed by the caravans of ivory from the interior passes, as I have said before, near Bembe; consequently a good many caravans left the usual track and came there to sell their ivory, or if they could not agree on the terms, passed on to the coast, and it was interesting to see them arrive, and watch the process of bartering.

From Bembe we could descry the long black line of negroes composing the "Quibucas" or caravans, far away on the horizon across the mine valley, and it was here that I became convinced of the superiority of the negro's eyesight over the white man's. Our blacks, particularly old Pae Tomás, could tell with the naked eye the number of tusks, and the number of bags of "fuba" or meal, in a caravan, and whether they brought any pigs or sheep with them, at such a distance that not one of us could distinguish anything without a glass—in fact, when we could only see a moving black line. Caravans of 200 and 300 natives, bringing as many as 100 large tusks of ivory, were not unfrequent.

As soon as they came within hearing distance, they beat their "Engongui," as the signal bells are called, one of which accompanies every "Quibuca," and is beaten to denote their approach, the towns answering them in the same manner, and intimating whether they can pass or not, if there is war on the road, and so on. These "Engongui" ([Plate IV.](#)) are two flat bells of malleable iron joined together by a bent handle, and are held in the left hand whilst being beaten with a short stick. There is a regular code of signals, and as each bell has a different note, a great number of variations can be produced by striking each alternately, or two or three beats on one to the same, or lesser number on the other; a curious effect is also produced by the performer striking the mouths of the bells against his naked stomach whilst they are reverberating from the blows with the stick.

As the caravans were coming down the valley, Pae Tomás used to amuse himself sometimes by signalling "war," or that the road was stopped, when the whole caravan would squat down, whilst the "Capatas," or head-men in charge, would come on alone, but at the signal "all right," or "road clear," all would start forward again.

Only one "Engongui" can be allowed in each town, and belongs to the king, who cannot part with it on any account, as it is considered a great "fetish," and is handed down from king to king. To obtain the one in my possession, I had to send Pae Tomás to the "Mujolo" country, where they are principally made, but as he was away only four days, I believe he must have got it nearer Bembe than the "Mujolo," which lies to the N.N.E. of Bembe, but according to all accounts at many days' journey, which I am inclined to believe, as these "Mujolos" never come down to the coast, and were formerly very rarely brought as slaves in the caravans. They are greatly prized as slaves by the Portuguese, as they are very strong and intelligent, and work at any trade much better than any other race in Angola. They have very peculiar square faces, and are immediately known by their cheeks being tattooed in fine perpendicular lines, in fact the only race in Angola that tattoo the face at all. They are said to be a very savage race, and to practise cannibalism.

When the caravans approached Bembe, the "Capatas" would dress themselves in their best and each carry an open umbrella, or when the "Capata" was a very important personage, the umbrella used to be carried before him by a black, whilst he followed behind in the sun.

The day of their arrival was always spent in looking over the stock of goods, and receiving presents of cloth and rum, and generally a pig for a feast. The next day the tusks would be produced and the barter arranged in the manner explained in the preceding chapter.

The caravans seldom brought any curiosities, only very rarely a few mats or skins; one skin that I purchased proved to be that of a new monkey, described by Dr. P. L. Sclater as the *Colobus Angolensis* ('Proceedings of the Zoological Society of London,' May, 1860).

A few slaves were sometimes brought to Bembe from the interior, and sold to the Cabinda blacks, who were our washer-boys, and also to the Ambriz men, our servants, slaves being amongst the natives in Angola the principal investment of their savings. The prices paid for them varied according to size, sex, age, and freedom from blemish or disease, and ranged from one to two pieces of "chilloes" (a Manchester-made cloth, in pieces of fourteen yards, and costing about 3*s.* each) for a boy or girl; to six or seven pieces, at most, for a full-grown man or woman.

Gum Elemi, called "Mubafo," used to be brought in large cakes, and is said to be very abundant not many days' journey from Bembe, but its low price in Europe does not allow of its becoming an article of trade from this part of Africa at present.

There are no cattle from the River Congo to the latitude of Loanda. At Bembe a few oxen used to arrive from a country eight to ten days' journey off, in a S.E. direction, but, although carefully tended, would gradually lose flesh and die in a few months. On the coast they seem to thrive very well in the hands of white men, but yet the natives never breed them, whether from indolence, or from the climate not being quite suitable to them, it is difficult to say, but most likely from the former.

The Portuguese expedition to occupy Bembe took mules, donkeys, and camels from the Cape de Verde Islands, but they all died, though in charge of a veterinary surgeon, who attributed their death to the character of the grass, most of the species having the blades very serrated, and according to him causing death by injury to the coats of the stomach.

In connection with the mortality of cattle and other animals, I may mention that all the cats at Bembe had their hind quarters more or less paralysed, generally when a few months old, sometimes even when quite young kittens, when it certainly could not be the result of any blow. This was the case without exception during the two years I was at Bembe. I have seen the same occur on the coast, but more rarely.

Sheep and goats breed very well, particularly about Ambrizzette. The sheep are a very peculiar variety, long-legged, and covered with short hair. The goats are small but especially beautiful, and generally black and white in colour. Cocks and hens are small and tasteless and always scarce, as the natives are too indolent to rear any, only keeping a few animals that can find their own living: they never think of giving them any food or water unless they are actually dying, the consequence is that only sheep and goats and a few fowls thrive or are seen in their towns. I have only seen a few pigeons in two or three towns. Their pigs, as might be imagined, are painful to look upon, living on grass and what few roots they can grub up, and on all the excrement and filth of the towns. It is impossible to conceive anything more distressingly thin and gaunt than the poor pigs, perfectly flat, and hardly able to trot along.

On our journey to Bembe the natives were greatly surprised at our giving some boiled rice from our plates to a brood of pretty little chickens at a town where we breakfasted, as they did not belong to us. Their dogs, wretched, small, starved, long-eared animals, like little jackals, live, like the pigs, upon rubbish, and hunt rats and other small game. I once saw a dog eating the grains off a green indian-corn cob, which he was holding down with his two front paws, nibbling it as a sheep would, and seeming to enjoy it. Cats are very rarely seen in the towns;—they are greatly esteemed by the Mushicongos for food, and their skins for wearing as an ornament. I once shot a half-wild cat that used to visit my fowl-yard, and had eaten some chickens; my cook skinned it, and sold the flesh for 300 beads, and the skin for 200—300 beads being then a fancy price for the largest fowl, ordinary chickens usually averaging 100 beads each only.

Provisions at that time were fabulously cheap, though not more so, perhaps, than should be expected from the wonderful fertility of the soil, the little trouble the natives have in its cultivation, and their small necessities. Eggs and bananas were sold at one blue glass bead each, of a kind made in Bohemia, and costing wholesale under twopence for a bunch of 600. Mandioca-meal, beans, &c., were sold at a similar rate.

One ugly black was the principal purveyor of eggs; he used to collect them at all the towns and fairs around, and bring them into Bembe for sale, but he was a sad rogue, and never sold a basketful of eggs but a number were sure to be found rotten. At the fort he was once tied over a gun and well thrashed, but this did not cure him, and at last, tired of buying bad eggs from him, I had him held by a couple of our servants the next time he brought me a basket of eggs for sale, whilst my cook broke them into a basin one by one, the rotten ones being rubbed on his great woolly head, on which he had allowed the hair to grow like a great frizzled bush. His appearance when released was most comical, and produced the greatest excitement among the rest of the niggers, who danced and yelled and hooted at him as he ran along, crying, to the stream at the mines to wash himself. The cure was effectual this time, and we never had further cause of complaint against him.

There are four weekly fairs or markets held near Bembe, the principal one being at Sona, about six miles off. To this market natives from many miles distant come with produce, &c., to barter for cloth, rum, and beads from the coast. To travel two or three days to attend a fair is thought nothing of by the blacks,—this is not to be wondered at when we consider the climate, and that a mat to sleep on is the most they need or carry with them on a journey. Their food being almost entirely vegetable and uncooked, they either take it with them, or buy it on the road.

Another celebrated fair is at Quimalenço, on the road to Bembe, and about thirty miles distant, and our servants and blacks working at the mine were constantly asking leave to go to it. Both at Sona and the latter fair no blacks are allowed with sticks or knives, a very wise precaution, considering the quantity of palm wine, garapa, and other intoxicating liquors consumed. I have seen not less than 2000 natives assembled at these fairs, selling and buying beans, mandioca roots and meal of different kinds, Indian corn, ground-nuts, palm-nuts and oil; pigs, sheep, goats, fowls; cotton cloth, handkerchiefs, &c.; crockery, clay pipes, and pipe-stems, but not a single article manufactured by themselves, with the exception, perhaps, of a few sleeping-mats, and the conical open baskets called "Quindas," in which the women carry roots, meal, and other produce on their heads.

During my first stay in Bembe, the king of Congo having died, his successor, the Marquis of Catende, came in state to Bembe to ask the Portuguese to send priests to San Salvador, to bury his predecessor and to crown him king. In former times, San Salvador, the capital of the kingdom of Congo, was the chief missionary station of the Portuguese, who built a cathedral and monasteries there, the ruins of which still exist; they appear to have been very successful in civilizing the natives, and though the mission was abandoned more than a hundred years ago, their memory is revered in the country to this day. I have been told by the Portuguese priests and officers who have been at San Salvador that the graves of the former missionaries are still carefully tended and preserved, with every sign of respect, and that missals and other books, letters, chalices, and other church furniture of the olden time still exist, and the natives would not part with them on any account.

In times past the King of Congo was very powerful; all the country, as far as and including Loanda, the River Congo, and Cabinda, was subject to him, and paid him tribute. The missionaries under his protection worked far and wide, attained great riches, and were of immense benefit to the country, where they and the Portuguese established and fostered sugar-cane plantations, indigo manufacture, iron smelting, and other industries. With the discovery and colonization of the Brazils, however, and the expulsion of the Jesuits from Angola, the power of the Portuguese and of the king of Congo has dwindled away to its present miserable condition. The king of Congo is now only the chief of San Salvador and a few other small towns, and does not receive the least tribute from any others, nor does he possess any power in the land. Among the natives of Angola, however, he still retains a certain amount of prestige as king of Congo, and all would do homage to him in his presence, as he is considered to possess the greatest "fetish" of all the kings and tribes, though powerless to exact tribute from them.

The Marquis came to Bembe attended by a retinue of 300 blacks and his private band, consisting of eight elephant tusks blown like horns, and six drums. These tusks were moderate sized, about three to three and a half feet long, and were bored down the centre nearly to the point, to a small hole, or narrow aperture cut in the side, to which the lips are applied to produce the sound, which is deep and loud, but soft in tone, and can be heard at a great distance. The drums are hollowed out of one piece of wood, generally of the "Mafumeira" tree, which is very soft and easily worked: the open end is covered with a sheepskin tightly stretched and rubbed over with bees-wax, a small portion of which is left sticking in the middle. Before use, these drums are slightly warmed at a fire to soften the wax and make the skin a little sticky, when being struck by the flat of the fingers (not the palms of the hands) they adhere slightly, and cause the blows to produce a more resonant sound. The better made ones are rubbed quite smooth on the outside with the dry leaf of a certain tree, which is very rough, and acts like sand-paper, and then dyed a bright red with the fresh red pulp enveloping the seeds of the Annatto plant (*Bixa Orellana*), which I have seen growing wild in the interior.

When the Marquis approached Bembe he made known his coming by his band blowing the horns and thumping the drums, and we could see the caravan in the distance slowly winding through the grass. On arriving at the edge of the mine valley they all halted, and the band again struck up. The Marquis got out of his hammock, attired like any other black, unlocked a small box containing his wardrobe, and proceeded to dress himself, in which operation he was assisted by his two secretaries;—first he put on a white shirt, but not having taken the precaution to unbutton the front, it was some time before his head emerged from it; a gaily-coloured cloth was next produced from the box and fastened round his waist; a blue velvet cloak edged with gold lace was put on his shoulders, and on his head a blue velvet cap, which completed his royal costume; his feet bare of course.

They then came into Bembe, and proceeded to the fort, where they were received with a salute of four guns, which it was the Marquis's right to receive from the Portuguese, but which being evidently unexpected, made one half of the crowd scamper as fast as they could, till they were recalled. At the gate the guard turned out and presented arms, and, preceded by the band of the fort, he was taken to the Governor's quarters, where we were all assembled to meet him.

The usual complimentary speeches then took place, his secretary translating for him, and the Governor's cook being interpreter on our side. The Marquis spoke only a few words of Portuguese, and never having been among white men, he was rather strange to the use of knives and forks, so at dinner his meat was cut up small for him, which he forked slowly into his mouth, now and then draining a whole tumblerful of Lisbon wine. The dinner-service of crockery and glass, &c., seemed to strike him as being of marvellous magnificence.

After first tasting a glass of beer myself, according to the fashion of the country, I offered it to him, to see how he would like it; he took a mouthful, but immediately turned round and spat it out, with a very wry face. He passed the remainder to his two secretaries, who were squatted on the ground behind him, eating stewed fowl and mandioca-meal out of a dish with their fingers. As it would have been an unpardonable incivility on their part not to drink whatever he gave them, they each took a mouthful from the glass, though he was making faces and wiping his mouth with the sleeve of his shirt, but both got up instantly and hurried outside, where we could hear them spitting and sputtering at the bitter draught.

On handing round the "palitos" or toothpicks after dinner, he took one, but did not know what to do with it till he saw to what use they were applied by us, when he burst out laughing, and said in Congo language, "that the white men were very strange people, who, after putting such delicious food into their mouths, must needs pick out the little bits from their teeth with a stick," and he asked for a few, which he gave to his secretaries to keep, to take back to his country as curiosities.

He is a handsome, stout, middle-aged man, and with a very much better cast of countenance than is usual among the Mushicongos.

During the time that he was at Bembe, the kings of the neighbouring towns came together one morning to pay him homage, and his state reception was a very amusing and interesting ceremony.

The kings and their people appeared, not in their best, but in the poorest and most ragged condition possible, whether according to custom, or from a fear that the Marquis might, in view of their riches, demand tribute from them as formerly, I know not. The Marquis was seated on a chair placed on a large mat, with his bare feet on a leopard skin;—behind his chair squatted the whole of his retinue.

The kings, with their people, not less than 100 blacks, on arriving at some little distance, dropped on their knees, bowed their heads to the ground, and then clapped their hands, to which the Marquis replied by moving the fingers of his right hand to them; one of his secretaries, a very tall, lanky negro, dressed in a quaker coat with a very high, straight collar, then knelt before him, and presented him with the sword of state, which the Marquis pulled out of the scabbard and returned to him.

The tall secretary now borrowed a red cloak from one of the retinue, which he secured round his waist with his left hand, allowing it to drag behind him like a long red tail, and commenced a series of most extraordinary antics, dancing about brandishing his sword, and pretending to cut off heads, to exemplify the fate in store for his majesty's enemies.

Approaching the kneeling embassy, he shook his sword at them like a harlequin at a clown in a pantomime, when they all rose and followed him for a few paces, and then dropped on their knees whilst he went through the dance and sword exercise again; this performance repeated, brought them nearer the Marquis, and a third time brought the whole lot to his feet, where they all rubbed their foreheads and fingers in the dust, whilst the secretary knelt and placed the sword across his knees; then came a general clapping of hands, and the king of Matuta and several others made long speeches, to which the Marquis replied, not to them directly, but to his secretary, who repeated it, every twenty or thirty words being interrupted by a great blowing of the horns and beating of the drums, lasting for a couple of minutes.

After the speeches the kings presented their offering, which consisted only of a gourd of palm wine, of which, according to custom, the Marquis had to drink.

The Governor of Bembe had provided him with a couple of bottles of Lisbon wine for the ceremony, and also a tumbler; this last was filled with palm wine from the gourd, and given to the secretary, and he handed it to the Marquis, who made the sign of the cross over it with his hand, repeating at the same time some words in Latin: this they have learnt from the ceremonies of the mass in the old Roman Catholic missals still in their possession.

The Marquis, not feeling inclined to drink palm wine, availed himself of the custom of the kings of Congo not eating or drinking in public, to practise a little deception. Whilst two attendants held up a large mat before him, he passed the tumblerful of palm wine to his secretaries, who quickly swallowed its contents, and taking up one of the bottles of Lisbon wine from under his chair, put it to his mouth, and nearly emptied it at a draught. The curtain was then removed, and the nearly empty bottle of wine passed to the king of Matuta, who poured the contents into the tumbler, took a drink himself, and passed it to the rest, who had a sip each till it was drained dry. Speeches were again made, and the embassy, having once more rubbed their foreheads and fingers in the dust, got up and bent nearly double, then turned and walked away very slowly and carefully, reminding me most comically of cats after they have been fighting.

A singular custom of the kings of Congo is that of never expectorating on the ground in public, it being "fetish" to do so, and foretelling some calamity. When the Marquis wished to clear his throat, the lanky secretary would kneel before him, and taking a dirty rag out of a grass pouch suspended from his shoulder, would present it to him with both his hands, to spit into; the rag was then carefully doubled up, kissed, and replaced in the pouch.

I was told by the padre at Bembe, who went on a mission to Engoge, that the king there, the "Dembo Ambuilla," also has the same custom, but performed in a much more disgusting manner, as, instead of spitting into a rag like the King of Congo, the "Dembo" expectorates into the palm of an attendant's hand, who then rubs it on his head!

Having heard at Loanda that Dr. Bastian had passed through San Salvador, I inquired of the Marquis whether he had seen him. He replied that a white man, whose name he knew not, had lately been through his town (a little distance from San Salvador), and had given him a "mucanda" or letter, which he would show me: and, taking me into his hut, he took out of his box a parcel of rags, which he carefully undid till he came to a half-sheet of small paper, on which was engraved the portrait of some British worthy dressed in the high-collared coat in fashion some thirty or forty years ago. As the lower half of the sheet was torn off, there was no inscription on it by which I could identify the portrait, which seemed to have been taken from a small octavo volume. The Marquis would not show the portrait to the Governor or any Portuguese, as he was afraid that it might say something that would compromise him with them, and on my assuring him that there was no danger whatever in it, he seemed to be much easier in his mind.

On the Sunday morning the Marquis attended the garrison's military mass, and caused much amusement by bringing his band with him, which played during the service. Although he had never before heard mass, his conduct, and that of the head men who accompanied him, was most proper and decorous; they knelt, crossed themselves, and seemed to pray as earnestly as if they had been brought up to it all their lives.

A visit they paid the works at the mines greatly interested them, the steam-engine and saw-mill specially attracting their attention; but the most incomprehensible wonder to them was an ordinary monkey, or screw-jack, which was fixed under one end of a huge trunk of a tree lying on the ground, and on which as many blacks were asked to sit as it could carry;—great was their astonishment to see me lift the whole tree and blacks by simply turning the handle of the monkey. After much clapping of their hands to their mouths, the universal way of expressing surprise by the blacks, the Marquis asked, through his tall secretary, how I had performed the wonderful "fetish?" I explained as well as I could, that it was due to the mechanism inside, but I could see they did not believe me, and I afterwards ascertained that they thought the power was contained in the handle.

The king only spoke a few words of Portuguese, but the tall secretary not only spoke, but wrote it very fairly. He assured me that he had not been taught by the white men, but by blacks whose ancestors had acquired the language from the old missionaries. I am inclined to believe that he must have been a native of Ambaca, or some other province of the interior of Angola, where a great many of the natives at the present day can read and write Portuguese, transmitted from father to son since the olden time.

Some time after the Marquis left, the Portuguese sent a padre from Loanda to join the one at Bembe, and proceed together to San Salvador, with an escort in charge of the officer at Bembe, an ignorant man, who, after the old king had been buried, became frightened and suddenly decamped without allowing them to crown the Marquis of Catende. A second expedition of 100 soldiers was then sent. The priests were welcomed with demonstrations of the greatest joy by the natives, who loaded them with presents; but the military were coldly received, and not a single present was given to them or the officer in command, who, alarmed at their hostility and vexed at the reception given to the padres, again retreated to Bembe as fast as he could, and to screen his want of success and cowardice, intrigued with the Governor-General at Loanda, and the padres were censured for that for which he himself was alone to blame.

Nearly 200 blacks presented themselves to the padres, saying that they were the descendants of the slaves of the former missionaries, and offering to rebuild the church and monasteries, if they were only directed and fed.

Had the Portuguese allowed the padres to go to San Salvador alone, unaccompanied by a military force, which gave an air of conquest to the expedition, a great step would have been made in the introduction of trade and civilization in that part of the interior, and it would have opened the way to geographical discovery. I am convinced that the invincible opposition to Lieutenant Grandy's passage into the interior was due principally to the fear of the natives that the Portuguese might follow in his steps, and annex the country from whence they derive their ivory.

The soil about Bembe is magnificent, and will produce almost anything. Sugar-cane grows to a huge size, and vegetables flourish in a remarkable manner. During the time I was there I had a fine kitchen-garden, and not only kept the miners supplied with vegetables, but almost every day sent as much as one, and sometimes two, blacks could carry to the fort for the soldiers. Greens of all kinds and cabbages grow beautifully, although the latter seldom form a hard head; all kinds of salad grow equally well, such as endive, lettuce, radishes, mustard and cress, &c.; peas, turnips, carrots, mint, and parsley also flourish, and tomatoes, larger than I ever saw them even in Spain and Portugal. Cucumbers, melons, and vegetable-marrows, we obtained very fine the first season, but the succeeding year a swarm of very small grasshoppers prevented us from getting a single one. Broad beans, although growing and flowering luxuriantly, never produced pods. I gave seeds to the old King of Matuta, and promised to buy their produce from him, and we very quickly had a load of beautiful vegetables every day.

It is almost impossible to estimate the advantage, in a country and climate like Africa, of an abundant supply of fresh salad and vegetables, and yet, although growing so luxuriantly, and with so small an amount of trouble, they are never cultivated by the natives of any part of Angola, and rarely by the Portuguese; the market at Loanda, for instance, is very badly supplied with vegetables.

Benguella and Mossamedes—particularly the latter—are the only exceptions to the general and stupid want of attention to the cultivation of vegetables. The only vegetable introduced by the former missionaries that still exists in cultivation in the country is the cabbage, which is sometimes seen in the towns (generally as a single plant only), growing with a thick stem, which is kept closely cropped of leaves, and as much as four or five feet high, surrounded by a fence to keep the goats and sheep from browsing on it; but I have never seen it in their plantations.

About Bembe a handsome creeper (*Mucuna pruriens*), with leaves like those of a scarlet-runner, and bearing large, long bunches of dark maroon bean-like flowers, grows very abundantly. The flowers are succeeded by crooked pods covered with fine hairs (cow-itch) which cause the most horrible itching when rubbed on the skin. The first time I pulled off a bunch of the pods I shook some of the hairs over my hand and face, and the sensation was alarming, like being suddenly stung all over with a nettle. I have seen blacks, when clearing bush for plantations, shake these hairs on their hot, naked bodies, and jump about like mad, until they were rubbed with handfuls of moist earth.

I saw at Bembe a striking illustration of the immunity of Europeans from fever and ague when travelling or otherwise actively employed.

One hundred Portuguese soldiers having misconducted themselves in some way at Loanda, were ordered to Bembe as a punishment. They marched from Ambriz in the worst part of the rainy season without tents (which, singular to say, are never used in Angola by the Portuguese troops), and were a fortnight in reaching Bembe.

They were not a bad-looking set of men, and were well shod and clothed, but had been badly fed on the road, principally on beans and mandioca-meal, and had had only water from the swollen pools and rivers to drink. Notwithstanding the exposure and hardships, only twelve fell ill on the march, and of those, only four or five had to be brought into Bembe in hammocks.

Fine barracks at the fort had been prepared for them, but next morning, on inspection by the doctor, no less than forty were ordered into hospital; next day thirty more followed, and within a week of their arrival every one of the 100 men had passed through the doctor's hands, suffering principally from attacks of intermittent fever and ague, remittent fever, and a few cases of diarrhœa; but, to show the comparatively healthy climate of Angola, only one man died.

We were not so fortunate with our Cornish miners, all fine, strong, healthy, picked men; several causes contributed to their ill-health and deaths;

exposure to sun and wet whilst at work, bad lodging, but principally great want of care on their part in eating and drinking whilst recovering from an attack of illness.

One circumstance that struck the doctor greatly, was the total want of pluck in the Cornishmen when ill; they used actually to cry like children, and lie down on their beds when suffering from only a slight attack of fever that a Portuguese would think nothing of. When they were seriously ill, it was with the greatest difficulty we could make them keep up their spirits, which is so essential to recovery, in fevers particularly. When convalescent, on the contrary, they could not be kept from eating or drinking everything, however indigestible or objectionable, that came in their way; and often was our good doctor vexed, and obliged to employ the few words of abuse he knew in English, on finding them, after a serious illness, eating unripe bananas, or a great plateful of biscuit and cheese and raw onions.

So constant were their relapses, from want of the commonest care on their part, that the doctor at last refused to attend them unless they were placed under lock and key till fit to be let out and feed themselves. Their complaints and grumblings, when well even, were incessant, and they were the most unhandy set imaginable; they could not even mend a broken bedstead, or put up a hook or shelf to keep their things from the wet or rats. There was but one exception, a boiler-maker, named Thomas Webster, who was a universal favourite from his constant good-humour and willingness. Poor fellow! after recovering from a very severe attack of bilious fever, he died at Ambriz, whilst waiting for the steamer that was to take him home.

The worthy Portuguese officer in command at Bembe on my last visit, Lieutenant Vital de Bettencourt Vasconcellos Canto do Corte Real, had prepared for our use the old house in which I had formerly lived, and received us most hospitably. We breakfasted and dined with him for the eight days of our stay, and with Lieutenant Grandy and his brother, who were also his guests. We were all the more thankful for Lieutenant Vital's very kind reception, from our cook having fallen ill the day before we arrived, and being consequently unable to prepare our food.

PLATE IX.
BEMBE PEAK.

We made several excursions to the mines and to the caves, and one morning my wife and myself ascended to the top of the peak or mountain (Plate IX.), and breakfasted there.

On the 15th April, 1873, we bade good-bye to Bembe, and to the brothers Grandy and Lieutenant Vital, who accompanied us to the River Luqueia. On the third day we arrived at Quiballa, where we remained four days, employing them, as before, in collecting butterflies and drying some fine plants, amongst others the beautiful large red flowers almost covering a fine tree (*Spathodea campanulata*—R. de B.?).

The second afternoon we were visited by a terrific thunderstorm; one vivid flash of lightning was followed almost instantaneously by a deafening clap of thunder; the former must have struck the ground very near our hut, as both my wife and myself felt a slight shock pass through our ankles quite distinctly, and on asking the owner of the hut and one of our blacks who were with us, if they had felt anything, they both described having felt the same sensation.

So much rain fell during this storm that we were forced to remain a couple of days longer, as some carriers had been obliged to return to Quiballa, unable to pass the rivers. It was now nearly the end of the rainy season, when the heaviest falls occur, and we had already, after leaving Bembe, found that a lovely bank on the River Lifua, on our journey up the country, had been swept away by a flood, and a high pile of sand covered the beautiful carpet of flowers and ferns.

A small dog that we had taken a fancy to on board the steamer in which we went out, and who had been our constant companion, also accompanied us on this journey, and it was amusing to see her attempts to swim the swift currents, where she generally had to be carried across. The faithful creature seemed to know that there was danger in crossing the swollen streams, and she would yelp and cry on the bank till my wife and myself had been carried over, when she would express her delight by tearing along the banks and paths like mad.

Her solicitude for our safety was sometimes rather embarrassing, as whenever she had passed a swamp, in which her legs generally sank deep into the black mud, she would always insist on jumping up on the hammocks, evidently to ascertain that we were all right, and of course quite unmindful of the dreadful mess she made with her wet paws.

Like all European dogs, she never got over a certain antipathy to the black race, and although on the best terms with our own boys, who delighted in petting her, she always showed her contempt for the natives by making sudden rushes at them, from under her mistress's hammock, when in passing through a town the women and children came running along cheering and shouting, to see the "white woman." Though she never bit them, her sudden and fierce-looking attack would generally scatter the crowd, who, however, always took it in good part. At night we always put her under the Madeira chair, which made a very good kind of cage, and which we placed at the foot of our bed under the mosquito curtain, thus saving her from these pests, and also preventing her from rushing out at any noise outside the tent.

The evening before we reached Quingombe, we raced the blackest thunderstorm I have ever witnessed. About four o'clock in the afternoon of the very fierce, hot and sultry day, the wind began to lull and distant thunder was heard behind us. The sky indicated plainly that no ordinary storm was gathering, the clouds deepening in colour till at last they seemed to descend and touch the ground, forming a nearly black curtain, which as it slowly advanced hid hills, trees, and everything behind it; the top part of this thick black curtain seemed to travel at a faster rate than the rest below, and slowly formed a black arch over-head; at about five o'clock it seemed to be only a few hundred yards behind us, like a solid angry night trying to overtake us. Sudden flashes and long streaks of lightning seemed to shoot out of it, up and down and in all directions, with scarcely any intermission of the explosions of thunder that accompanied them.

Our carriers seemed perfectly frightened, and ran us along in our hammocks as if racing for life, till, a little before sunset, we reached a small village near the road, just as the advancing raindrops at last overtook and began pattering down upon us. We hurried with our baggage into a hut, but the wind suddenly seemed to increase in power from the south, and blew the storm away from its path to the westward, so that it only rained for about half an hour, and we had just time to set up our tent before the darkness of night, calm and cool, came on. Some of our carriers, who had remained behind and not been able to keep ahead of the storm, described the rain as coming down on them like a perfect deluge.

Next day we arrived late in the afternoon at Quingombe, and our carriers tried to dissuade us from proceeding on to Ambriz, alleging that the heavy rains had filled the marshes, so that they were impassable in the dark; but disbelieving them, I hurried them on, and reached the swamp that separates the town of Quingombe from the ferry on the River Loge at Quincollo;— sure enough it was one sheet of water, but unwilling to brave another night of mosquitoes we pushed on. Twice we had to get out of our hammocks (which were slung as high as they could possibly be) on to the Madeira chair, to be carried across deep places; and for about two miles there was hardly a dry place, our poor dog swimming and carried most of the time.

At last, at seven in the evening, we arrived at Quincollo to find that the river had overflowed the banks, and that, with the exception of a house and cane-mill, there was not a foot of dry ground to encamp upon, except a great heap of cane refuse from the mill. This and the house belonged to a convict, who had been a swineherd in Portugal, but in consequence of the abolition of capital punishment in that country, had escaped hanging, after committing a cruel murder. He is now a large slaveholder, agent to the line of steamers from Lisbon owned by an English firm at Hull, and much protected by the Portuguese authorities at Loanda!

Not caring to sleep on his premises, we encamped on the heap of refuse, on which we found it impossible to put up our tent, contenting ourselves with hanging up the mosquito-bar alone. We had reached our last biscuit and tin of preserved provision, and had just finished our tea and supper when the white man in charge of the convict's premises, with his servants, came out with torches and armed, to find out who we were, fearing it might be an attack of the natives of Quingombe. He was most kind and pressing in his offers of shelter, in the absence of the owner, but we declined. He made us promise, however, that we would accept a canoe of his in the morning, which took us down the river about six miles to the bar, from whence we rode in our hammocks along the beach to Ambriz, thus happily ending our last excursion in Africa.

We had been absent just one month, in the worst part of the rainy season, without the slightest illness, and returned laden with a very interesting collection of insects and plants.

CHAPTER VIII.
CHARACTER OF THE NEGRO—FETISH—CUSTOMS—ARMS AND WAR—DRESS—ZOMBO TRIBE—BURIAL—INSANITY.

The language, customs, and habits of the Mussurongo, Ambriz, and Mushicongo tribes are very similar, and are distinguished in many particulars from those of the natives of the district of Loanda, who speak the Bunda language. This is not astonishing, when we consider that Loanda has been constantly occupied by the white race since its discovery, and that this intercourse has necessarily modified their character to a certain extent. The former tribes are, however, still almost in their primitive or natural condition, and should be studied or described apart and before continuing the description of the country south of about 8°, their limit in latitude.

I believe that it is very difficult to understand correctly the character of the negro race in Africa, and that it requires long intercourse with, and living amongst them, to get behind the scenes, as it were, and learn their manner of thought or reasoning, and in what way it influences their life and actions.

In the first instance, it is not easy to dispossess oneself of the prejudices both against and in favour of the negro. It is so natural to judge him by our own standard, and as we should wish him to be;—so easy to think of him as agreeing with the preconceived idea that he is just like one of ourselves, but simply in a state of innocent darkness, and that we have only to show him the way for him to become civilized at once.

It is very disagreeable to find in the negro an entirely new and different state of things to that we had fondly imagined, and to have to throw overboard our cherished theories and confess our ignorance and that we have been entirely mistaken; but the truth must be told, and we shall have to run counter to the self-satisfied wisdom of the great number of people who judge from not always wilfully false reports, but from hasty or superficial descriptions or tales that agree with their foregone conclusions, and whose benevolent feelings and sympathy for the negro are therefore established upon baseless grounds.

It is not my intention to deprecate any efforts for the benefit of the negro race, but simply to show that the good seed in Africa *will* fall on bare and barren ground, and where weeds *will* rise and choke it; and I must warn philanthropy that its bounty is less productive of good results on the negro of tropical Africa than perhaps on any other race.

It is heartrending to see money, lives, and efforts squandered and wasted under the misguided idea of raising the negro to a position which, from his mental constitution, he cannot possibly attain, whilst so many of our own race are doomed from innocent infancy to grow up among us to a future of misery and vice, and when we know that the charity so lavishly shown to the negro and almost completely wasted would enable many of these poor children to become good and useful members of society. Let us, by all means, bring in the frozen vipers, and feed the famished wolves and the hungry vultures, but do not let us expect that because we have done so they will change into harmless snakes, noble dogs, or innocent doves, or neglect to succour the lambs and sheep of our own flock.

I cannot help thinking that so long as (in a rich country like England) we read of poor creatures perishing from starvation on doorsteps and in garrets, more care should be taken of our starving poor at home and less charity showered upon the negro, who has growing close to his hut all he wants to sustain life in almost absolute laziness.

The character of the negro is principally distinguished not so much by the presence of positively bad, as by the absence of good qualities, and of feelings and emotions that we can hardly understand or realize to be wanting in human nature. It is hardly correct to describe the negro intellect as debased and sunken, but rather as belonging to an arrested stage. There is nothing inconsistent in this; it is, on the contrary, perfectly consistent with what we have seen to be their physical nature. It would be very singular indeed if a peculiar adaptation for resisting so perfectly the malignant influences of the climate of tropical Africa, the result of an inferior physical organization, was unaccompanied by a corresponding inferiority of mental constitution. It is only on the theory of "Natural Selection, or the survival of the fittest" to resist the baneful influence of the climate through successive and thousands of generations—the "fittest" being those of greatest physical insensibility—that the present fever-resisting, miasma-proof negro has been produced, and his character can only be explained in the corresponding and accompanying retardation or arrest of development of his intellect.

The negro knows not love, affection, or jealousy. Male animals and birds are tender and loving to their females; cats show their affection by delicious purring noises and by licking; horses by neighing and pawing; cocks by calling their hens to any food they may find; parroquets, pigeons, and other birds, by scratching one another's polls and billing and cooing; monkeys by nestling together and hunting for inconvenient parasites on each other's bodies; but in all the long years I have been in Africa I have never seen a negro manifest the least tenderness for or to a negress. I have never seen a negro, even when inebriated, kiss a girl or ever attempt to take the least liberty, or show by any look or action the desire to do so. I have never seen a negro put his arm round a woman's waist, or give or receive any caress whatever that would indicate the slightest loving regard or affection on either side. They have no words or expressions in their language indicative of affection or love. Their passion is purely of an animal description, unaccompanied by the least sympathetic affections of love or endearment. It is not astonishing, therefore, that jealousy should hardly exist; the greatest breach of conduct on the part of a married woman is but little thought of. The husband, by their laws, can at most return his wife to her father, who has to refund the present he received on her marriage; but this extreme penalty is seldom resorted to, fining the paramour being considered a sufficient satisfaction. The fine is generally a pig, and rum or other drink, with which a feast is celebrated by all parties. The woman is not punished in any way, nor does any disgrace attach to her conduct. Adultery on the part of the husband is not considered an offence at all, and is not even resented by the wives.

It might be imagined that this lax state of things would lead to much immorality: but such is not the case, as from their utter want of love and appreciation of female beauty or charms, they are quite satisfied and content with any woman possessing even the greatest amount of the hideous ugliness with which nature has so bountifully provided them. Even for their offspring they have but little love beyond that which is implanted in all animals for their young. Mothers are very rarely indeed seen playing with or fondling their babies: as for kissing them, or children their mothers, such a thing is not even thought of. At the same time I have never seen a woman grossly neglect or abandon her child, though they think nothing of laying them down to sleep anywhere in the sun, where they soon become covered with flies; but as this does not appear to hurt or inconvenience them in the least, it can hardly be termed neglect.

The negro is not cruelly inclined; that is to say, he will not inflict pain for any pleasure it may cause him, or for revenge, but at the same time he has not the slightest idea of mercy, pity, or compassion for suffering. A fellow-creature, or animal, writhing in pain or torture, is to him a sight highly provocative of merriment and enjoyment. I have seen a number of blacks at Loanda, men, women, and children, stand round, roaring with laughter at seeing a poor mongrel dog that had been run over by a cart, twist and roll about in agony on the ground, where it was yelping piteously, till a white man put it out of its misery. An animal that does not belong to them, might die a thousand times of hunger and thirst before they would think of stirring a foot to give it either food or drink, and I have already described how even their own animals are left to fare and shift as best they can on their own resources, and their surprise that my wife should feed some little chickens that did not belong to her, at a town on the road to Bembe.

In the houses it is necessary to see for oneself that all the animals are regularly fed and watered every day, or they would quickly die of neglect. We cannot, therefore, be surprised to find the negro so completely devoid of vindictive feelings as he is. He may be thrashed to within an inch of his life, and not only recover in a marvellously short space of time, but bear no malice whatever, either at the time or afterwards. In Angola, the attempt to take a white man's life by his slaves, for ill treatment or cruelty to them, is extremely rare. If any amount of bad treatment is not resented, no benefit or good, however great, done to a negro, is appreciated or recognised by him: such a thing as gratitude is quite unknown to him; he will express the greatest delight at receiving a present or any benefit, but it is not from thankfulness; he only exhibits the pleasure he feels at having obtained it without an effort on his part. He cannot be called ungrateful exactly, because that would imply a certain amount of appreciation for favours conferred, which he does not feel. In the same way his constant want of truth, and his invariable dishonesty are the result, not so much of a vicious disposition, as of the impossibility to understand that there is anything wrong in being either a liar or a thief: that they are not vicious thieves is shown by the few concerted robberies practised by them, and the comparative safety of property in general; their thieving, as a rule, is more of a petty and pilfering description, in which, as might be expected, they are very cunning indeed.

To sum up the negro character, it is deficient in the passions, and in their corresponding virtues, and the life of the negro in his primitive condition, apparently so peaceful and innocent, is not that of an unsophisticated state of existence, but is due to what may be described as an organically rudimentary form of mind, and consequently capable of but little development to a higher type; mere peaceable, vegetarian, prolific human rabbits and guinea pigs, in fact; they may be tamed and taught to read and write, sing psalms, and other tricks, but negroes they must remain to the end of the chapter. The negro has no idea of a Creator or of a future existence; neither does he adore the sun nor any other object, idol, or image. His whole belief is in evil spirits, and in charms or "fetishes:" these "fetishes" can be employed for evil as well as to counteract the bad effect of other malign "fetishes" or spirits. Even the natives of Portuguese Angola, who have received the idea of God or Creator from the white men, will not allow that the same Power rules over both races, but that the God of the white man is another, and different from the God of the black man; as one old negro that I was once arguing with expressed it, "Your God taught you to make gunpowder and guns, but ours never did," and it is perfectly established in their minds that in consequence of our belonging to another and more powerful God, their "fetishes" are unavailing either for good or evil, to the white man; our ridiculing their belief in "fetish" only serves to make them believe the more in it.

In almost every large town there is a "fetish house" under the care of a "fetish man." This house is generally in the form of a diminutive square hut, with mud walls, painted white, and these covered with figures of men and beasts in red and black colours. The spirit is supposed to reside in this habitation, and is believed to watch over the safety of the town: the hut also contains the stock-in-trade of the "fetish man." These "fetish men" are consulted in all cases of sickness or death, as also to work charms in favour of, and against every imaginable thing; for luck, health, rain, good crops, fecundity; against all illness, storms, fire, surf, and misfortunes and calamities of every kind. No death is attributed to natural causes, it is always ascribed to the person or animal having been "fetished" by some spirit or living person, and the "fetish man" is consulted to find out, and if the latter, the culprit is fined, sold into slavery or executed, or has to take "casca," to prove his innocence. The "fetish man" also prepares the charms against sickness, &c., with which every man, woman, and child, as well as their huts and plantations, is provided.

These charms are of many kinds, and are worn round the neck and waist, or suspended from the shoulder. A short bit of wood with a carved head, with a couple of beads, cowries, or brass tacks for eyes, and contained in a little pouch, with the head left sticking out, and hung by a string round the neck, is a very common form. A pouch stuffed full of fowls' dung, feathers, and "tacula," is also a favourite "fetish." A bundle of rags or shreds of cotton cloth of all kinds, black with filth and perspiration, is often seen suspended from the shoulder or hung in their huts. The large flat seed of the "Entada gigantea" is also a common "fetish" to hang from the neck. A couple of iron bells like the "Engongui" described in page 203 but very much smaller, and with a small bit of iron as a clapper inside, are often hung from the neck or waist. Small antelopes' horns, empty or filled with various kinds of filth, are also suspended round the neck for charms. Children are never seen without a string tied round the waist, with or without some beads strung on it, and the ends hanging down in front. The land shells (*Achatina Welwitschii* and *Zebrina*) are filled with fowls' dung and feathers, "tacula," &c., and stuck on a stick in the plantations and salt pits, to protect them from thieves; also the gourd-like pods or fruit of the baobab tree, likewise filled with various kinds of filth, and painted on the outside white and red, with "pemba" (a white talcose earth from the decomposition of mica and mica schist) and "tacula." A great "fetish" in childbirth and infancy is made in the shape of a little pouch about two inches long and the thickness of the middle finger, very prettily woven of fine grass; these are filled with fowls' dung and "tacula," and a couple are placed in a small vessel containing water; the father of the child squeezes the pouches in the water, much in the manner that a washerwoman does her blue-bag, till it becomes coloured by the dirt and dye in the pouch; he then sprinkles the mother and newly-born child with the dirty water, and ties one of the pouches round the mother's neck, and the other round the child's. If this be not done, the blacks believe that the mother and child would quickly die;—the pouches are not taken off till the child can walk. Another great "fetish" in childbirth is a large bunch of a round hollow seed like a large marble, which is hung round the mother's neck, and not taken off till the child is weaned, generally in twelve moons, or a year's time.

Hung in the huts, and outside over the doors are all kinds of "fetishes," and in the towns and about the huts are various figures, generally roughly carved in wood, and sometimes made of clay, but always coloured red, black, and white. The finest "fetishes" are made by the Mussurongos on the Congo River. Plate IV. represents one obtained at Boma. Some of these large "fetishes" have a wide-spread reputation, and the "fetish men" to whom they belong are often sent for from long distances to work some charm or cure with them. I have constantly met them carrying these great ugly figures, and accompanied by two or three attendants beating drums and chanting a dismal song as they go along.

On the coast there are several "fetish men" who are believed to have power over the surf, and their aid is always invoked by the natives when it lasts long, or is so strong as to prevent them going out in their canoes to fish. There is a celebrated one at Musserra, and I have often seen him on the high cliff or point going through his incantations to allay the heavy surf; he has a special dress for the occasion, it being almost covered with shells and sea-weed; he is called the "Mother of the Water," and his power is held in great dread by the natives. No white man can go to the Granite Pillar at Musserra without having propitiated him by a present. This one, however, being half idiotic, is a poor harmless black, but others are not so, and render themselves very troublesome to the white traders by working mischief against them amongst the natives. A young Englishman established at Ambrizzette, although well known to them for many years, having been formerly engaged amongst them in the slave trade, was obliged to escape from there for a time, in consequence of an epidemic of small-pox being ascribed by the "fetish men" as having been introduced into the country by him, in a jar!

Others take advantage of the dread the natives have of spirits, to commit robberies. One at Bembe robbed several houses during the absence of the white owners, by mewing like a cat, when, such was the fear of the blacks, that they instantly lay on the ground, face downwards, and covered their heads till he had gone away; meantime he had coolly walked in and helped himself to whatever he pleased;—in this way he went off with a trunk full of clothes from the doctor's house, the servants not daring to lift up their heads as soon as they heard the mewing approaching, in the firm belief that they would be instantly struck dead if they even saw him. I heard this man mewing in the high grass behind my house one night, when I instantly fired a charge of small shot in the direction of the noise, and I did not hear him again till a few days after, when, having been captured by a Portuguese soldier whilst attempting to rob his hut, he was tied on a gun at the fort, and by a tremendous thrashing made to mew in earnest. All the blacks in the place went to see him punished, jeering at him, and telling him the white man's "fetish" was stronger than his.

The negroes have great confidence in the power of "fetishes" to protect their houses, &c., from fire or other misfortune, and an instance that I witnessed at Bembe proves their blind faith in them. The Cabinda negroes who were working as washer-boys, &c., lived apart from the other natives, as they always do, in a little town or collection of huts by themselves; one afternoon one of these huts caught fire, and such was their belief in their "Manipanzos" as they call their "fetish" figures, to preserve the huts from fire, that they did nothing either to put it out, or to prevent the flames spreading; in a very short time the town was consumed, and the Cabindas lost the whole of their property; they ran about like madmen, throwing up their arms and crying out, and abusing the "Endochi" (their name for Endoqui) in Cabinda who had cheated them with useless "fetishes," and vowed vengeance on him when they should return to their country.

The Mussurongo, Ambriz, and Mushicongo negroes, are much afraid of going about at night, unless there is moonlight; if one is sent with a message on a dark night, he always takes one or two more with him for protection, for fear of spirits.

As already noticed, when speaking of the present want of power of the King of Congo, there are no very great chiefs in the country from the River Congo to the district of Loanda, the most important or powerful being the King of N'Bamba and the "Dembo Ambuilla," or King of Encoge. Every town has its own king and council, generally of ten or twelve of the oldest men, who are called "Macotas," and who together administer the laws, settle disputes, &c. A king has no power by himself, the natives simply reverencing him as being invested with the "fetish" of chief, and he receives very little tribute from the natives of his own town; the fines and penalties levied he has also to divide with the "Macotas."

In all the tribes of Angola that I am acquainted with, the office of king descends from uncle to nephew (or in want of nephew, to niece), but by the sister's side, as, from what we call morals being but little understood by them, the paternity of any child is liable to very great doubt; but as a black once explained to me, "there is no doubt that my sister and myself came from the same mother, and there is no doubt, therefore, that my sister's child must be my nephew." This necessity for a positive or certain descent is very curious, as no record is kept of their pedigree or history.

The only division of time being into moons or months, and into dry and wet seasons, and no record of any kind being kept, blacks are quite unable to estimate their own age; servants keep an account of the months they are in service by tying a knot on a string for every moon.

Every king has a stick of office; this is in form like a straight, thick, smooth walking-stick, generally made of ebony, or of other wood dyed black, almost always plain, but sometimes carved with various patterns and ornamented with brass tacks, or inlaid with different designs in brass or tin plate. These sticks are always sent with a messenger from the king, and serve to authenticate the message. The principal insignia of the king's office is the cap, which is hereditary. It resembles a short nightcap, and is made of fine fibre, generally that of the wild pineapple leaf, and some are beautifully woven with raised patterns. The king never wears it in the usual way, but on any occasion of ceremony it is carried on the head doubled in four. The "Macotas" also use the same kind of cap, but worn properly on the head, and, like the king, only on occasions of ceremony.

When a white man, travelling, stops to rest for meals, or to sleep at a town, it is usual for the king and "Macotas" to give him a ceremonious reception, for which the king dresses himself in his best, and when they are all assembled they send word to say that they are ready to make their compliments. The meeting is generally in front of the king's hut, or else under the largest tree in the town (usually a baobab), where ceremonials have taken place from time immemorial. The king only is seated, another seat being placed at a little distance in front for the traveller. All the hammock-boys and servants belonging to the latter attend and squat behind him; on the king's side is generally the whole available population of the town, for whom the occasion is an excitement, the front rows squatting on the ground, and the rest standing crowded together in a circle. The traveller's retinue first begin by clapping hands to the king and "Macotas." This is performed in a peculiar manner by hollowing both palms, as in the action of filling them with water, and then bringing them together crosswise, when a much louder and deeper sound is produced than by clapping the hands in the ordinary manner. The king returns the salute by extending the left hand before him horizontally, with the palm towards him, and placing the back of the right hand flat in the palm of the left, and the fingers projecting over it are then waved quickly in succession in that position. (Plate V., figs. 5, 6.) This is the universal manner of greeting in Angola between an inferior and superior of high rank; when the difference is not so great, as children to their parents, slaves to their masters, ordinary natives to their "Macotas," &c., both clap their hands, but the inferior has to do it first, and both squat down for a moment to do it. A powerful king answers a salute by simply lifting his right hand, and waving his first and second finger only.

The king then speaks to one of the "Macotas" who can best translate his speech to the white man, welcoming him to the town, and inquiring after his health; the traveller then calls one of his attendants to act as interpreter, and returns the compliments, and makes the king a present of a few handkerchiefs and beads for his wives, but the ceremonial is not considered complete without the traveller presenting a bottle or a drink of wine or rum, which the king first partakes of, and then passes to the "Macotas;"—the white man then shakes hands with the king and takes his leave, the king always sending him some little present, generally a fowl or pig, for which, however, another present equal to its value is expected. It is not considered etiquette for the king to speak Portuguese on these occasions, however well he may know or understand it, but always to use his native language, and employ an interpreter; the white man must also employ an interpreter to translate his speech.

Besides rubbing the forehead on the ground to a powerful king, which I have described as practised to the King of Congo, the blacks have another way of rendering homage; this is by rubbing the fingers of both hands on the ground, and transferring the dust that adheres to them to the eyebrows, ears, and cheeks.

The appearance of some of the kings dressed in their fine clothes is very ridiculous. A red or blue baize cloak thrown over the shoulders is considered the correct thing, particularly over an old uniform of any kind, with the more gold lace on it the better. The old King of Quirillo, on the road to Bembe, was as amusing a figure as any I have seen. He always used to appear in a woman's brightly-coloured chintz gown, with a short red cloak over his shoulders, and a great brass cavalry helmet on his head, his black wrinkled face in a broad grin of satisfaction at the admiration that his brilliant costume appeared to excite among the natives.

The blacks in this part of the country are armed with flint muskets, of which many thousands are annually passed in trade on the coast. They like the heavy pattern of gun, unlike the natives to the south, who will only have very light flimsy Liege-made guns. They are fond of ornamenting the stock with brass tacks;—I have seen the whole of the woodwork of some of their muskets completely covered with them. They have no idea of using them properly, generally firing them from the side without any regard to aim or the distance that they can carry. Their manner of loading them I have already described.

These natives are arrant cowards, and in their so-called wars or disputes between one town and another they seldom resort to firearms to settle their differences. If one man is killed or wounded it is considered a very great war indeed, although a great deal of powder may have been burnt in mutual defiance at a safe distance. The Portuguese were engaged in war on several occasions on the road to Bembe, and punished, by burning, a number of towns where robberies had been committed, and where, from the thickness of the bush and forest, the ridiculously small force at their command would have been quickly massacred, had not the natives been such craven cowards, and so incapable of using their firearms. A shot from a six-pounder gun, by which a king and seven other blacks were killed—swept off a path where they were standing in file at what they considered a safe distance—contributed more than anything else to restore peace on the road.

The boats that used to navigate the River Congo were formerly armed with a small carronade, to protect themselves from any attack by the piratical Mussurongos on that river. One of these carronades falling into the hands of those blacks was by them sold to a town in the interior. The natives of this became involved in a dispute with those of a powerful neighbouring town, who proceeded to attack it. The natives of the former town, who depended on the carronade as their principal means of defence, placed it on the path, loaded to the muzzle with powder and stones, and laying a long train of powder to it awaited the advance of the enemy; when it appeared in sight the train was fired, and the inhabitants took to their heels. The assailing army, hearing such a terrific report, paused to consider, and prudently decided to return to their town. Next day they sent proposals of peace to the little town, saying that as the latter had such a big "fetish," they could not think of making war any more.

The Mussurongo and Ambriz blacks knock out the two middle front teeth in the upper jaw on arriving at the age of puberty. The Mushicongos are distinguished from them by having all their front teeth, top and bottom, chipped into points, which gives them a very curious appearance. These tribes, like all blacks, have magnificent sets of teeth, and the great care they take to keep them beautifully clean is most singular, considering their generally dirty habits and want of cleanliness. A negro's first care in the morning is to rinse out his mouth, generally using his forefinger to rub his teeth; the big mouthful of water with which they wash their mouths is always squirted out afterwards in a thin stream on their hands, to wash them with, this being about the extent of their ablutions. Many use a bit of cane switch or soft stick with the end beaten into a brush of fibres to clean their teeth with, this brush being often carried suspended from a piece of string round their necks. After every meal they always wash their mouths and teeth, and I have seen them dip their forefinger into the clean sharp sand of a river, and use it vigorously as tooth-powder.

Polygamy is of course an established institution among the natives of Angola, and the number of wives that a black may keep is only regulated by his means to maintain them. This applies to free blacks, the wives or married women being all free. A free man may also keep as many slaves and concubines as he can clothe.

There is no ceremony of marriage amongst the Mussurongo, Ambriz, or Mushicongo blacks, except mutual consent, but the bridegroom has to make his father-in-law a present of from two to three pieces of cloth and some bottles of rum. He has, besides, to provide a feast to which all the relatives of both families are invited, and in which a pig is an indispensable element, and as much rum or other drink as his means will allow. The bride's trousseau is also provided by him, but this, among the poorer Mushicongos, very often only consists of a couple of handkerchiefs or a fathom of cotton cloth. In many cases the bride is delivered over naked to the bridegroom. He has to provide her with clothing, baskets, hoe, pipe, pots for cooking, wooden platters, &c., and a separate hut with sleeping-mat for each wife; in return for this the wives have to cook and cultivate the plantations and to keep themselves and the husband in food. Should he be unable to supply a wife with the customary clothing, &c., she can leave him and return to her parents, in which case he loses her, and the amount he gave for her as well.

The dress of the blacks near the coast is, as might be expected, not so scanty as those farther inland. The men wear a waistcloth reaching to the knees, tied round the waist with a strip of red baize, and those who can afford it fringe the ends of the cloth, which are allowed to hang nearly to, and in some cases to trail on, the ground. The women sew together two widths of cotton cloth, which is worn wrapped round the body, covering it from under the arm-pits to the knees, and tied in the same manner round the waist with a strip of baize;—the top-end being tucked in, secures the cloth under the arms over the breast, but when travelling or working in the fields, they allow the top width to fall down on their hips, and leave the upper part of the body exposed. In the poorer towns the men only wear a small waistcloth of cotton cloth or matting; the women also wear a short waistcloth, and a handkerchief folded diagonally and tied tightly under the arms, with the ends hanging over and partly concealing the breasts. Girls and young women generally wear a single handkerchief tied by a string round their hips, the ends of the handkerchief not meeting at the side, leaving one thigh exposed. Children run about stark naked, or with a piece of string tied round the waist and the ends hanging down in front. Their covering at night is only the waistcloth or mat, which is generally long enough to cover them from head to foot. These mats are made from the cuticle of the leaves of a dwarf palm, which is peeled off when green and dried in the sun. It is only very few of the richer folks who have a baize cloth or other covering for their bodies at night. As might be expected, they are very glad to get cast-off garments, and they will wear any article of clothing however ragged it may be. One of my boys, to whom

I had given an old shirt without a back, fastened it on by lacing it up behind with a string, and the contrast presented by his shiny black back and his clean shirt front, collar, and sleeves, was most comical. Another hammock-boy made his appearance in a wide-awake, blue silk tie, pair of slippers, and the body-part of an old pair of white duck-trousers I had given him, the legs of which he had cut off to make a present of to his brother. The cotton umbrellas they receive in barter from the traders, each segment of which is a different bright colour, when old are taken off the ribs, the hole at the top is enlarged to pass the head through, and they are then worn on the shoulders like a cape.

The coast tribes do not interfere with nature in the development of the female figure, but the Mushicongos object to prominent breasts, and girls tie a string tightly round the chest to reduce the growing breasts to the perfectly flat shape in fashion;—the appearance of some of the old negresses with their breasts hanging low and flat in front is very disgusting.

The blacks have a great admiration for a white woman's costume, and I shall never forget an old "Capata's" description of a Portuguese officer's wife that he had seen at Ambriz, or his imitation of her slim waist and flowing dress. I told him I would send him a thin-waisted wife from England if he promised to put away the three he then had; he refused then, but next day came to me and said that, having considered my offer, he would accept it!

The Mussurongo, but not the Ambriz or Mushicongo men, wear ankle-rings made of brass (European make), or of tin, made by themselves from bar-tin obtained in trade from the white men. The women of the three tribes are very fond of wearing rings both on their arms and legs; these are sometimes made in one piece of thin brass wire wound loosely round the arm or leg, but a number of separate rings, about the size of ordinary rings on curtain-rods, is most esteemed, and they must be solid; they are not appreciated if hollow. Some of the richer women wear as many as twenty of these rings on each leg and arm, the weight rendering them almost unable to move, but six or eight is a very usual number to wear on each limb. It must not be understood that this is the universal custom, as it is only the wives of the kings or "Macotas" who can afford these ornaments.

These three tribes generally keep their heads shaved, or else only allow their hair to grow very short, and cut or shave it into various patterns, sometimes very complicated in character. Where razors or scissors are scarce, I have seen blacks shave heads with a piece of glass split from the bottom of an ordinary bottle, the operator stretching the skin of the scalp tightly towards him with the thumb of the left hand, while he scrapes away from him with the sharp edge of the wedge-shaped piece of glass in his right. Did they not keep their woolly heads so free from hair, great would be the production of a certain obnoxious insect, under the combined influence of dirt and heat. Amongst the Mushicongos the chiefs' wives and other more aristocratic ladies allow their hair to grow into a huge worsted-looking bush or mop, which is carefully combed straight up and out, and of course swarms with insect inhabitants. A very curious plan is adopted to entrap them:—a number of little flask-shaped gourds, about the size of an ordinary pear, are strung through their necks on a string, which is tied round the greasy forehead; a little loose cotton-wool is stuffed into each, and the open narrow ends stick into the bush of hair; they are taken off each morning, the cotton-wool is pulled out, and the little innocents that have crawled into it are crunched on the ground with a stone; the wool is replaced, and they are again hung round the back of the head as before. These traps in fact act in the same way as the little pots turned upside down and filled with hay, which our gardeners employ to capture earwigs on dahlias.

Hunting them by hand is of course very much in vogue, and I was once greatly amused at the way the chase was carried on on a woman's head at a town called Sangue, near Bembe. She was sitting on a low stool, and two girls were busily turning over her hair and collecting the lively specimens, which, as they were caught, were pinched to prevent their crawling, and placed in the open palm of a child's hand, who also stood in the group. My curiosity was excited as to the reason of the specimens being thus carefully preserved, and on asking one of my hammock-boys, he told me "that is for the payment"—they are afterwards counted, and the girls get a glass bead for every one they have caught.

I thought that a bead each was rather high pay for the work, and told him so; his answer was, "If you had a hundred on your head, would you not give a hundred beads to have them caught?" and I was obliged to confess that I should consider it a cheap riddance.

The Zombo and other natives farther to the interior, who come to the coast with ivory, &c., seldom shave their heads: the common lot let their hair grow anyhow, without apparently ever combing it out—a confused mass of wool, dirt, and palm oil—so that it gives them a wild appearance; others comb it straight up, letting it grow about six inches long, and ornament the front with a cock's feather or a red flower, or sometimes stick two or three brass tacks in it; others shave their heads all round, leaving the hair in the middle to grow upright, but the most usual manner is to plait their hair in little strings all over the head; some twist and plait these strings again round the head, ending at the top in a round knob, so that they look exactly as if they had a basket on their heads.

Any malformation with which a child may be born is considered a "fetish" by the negroes in Angola. A very short or sunken neck is thought a very great fetish indeed. I saw two blacks in the Bembe country who seemed to have no necks at all.

Albinos are not at all uncommon, and very repulsive looking creatures they are, with their dirty white, scabby, shrunken skins. Blacks with six fingers and toes are often seen, and are also considered as "fetish."

Women bear children with the greatest facility. In every town there are one or more old women who act as midwives, and I was informed that very few deaths indeed occur from childbirth, and in a very short time after the mothers may be seen about.

A very striking instance of the ease with which women go through this trial, happened to my knowledge whilst I was at Benguella. Senhor Conceição, the agent of the copper mine I was exploring there, had occasion to send up a number of poles to the mine, which was about six miles inland. He called his slaves together early one morning and told them that all who were able to carry poles should take up one and go off to the mine with it;—these wooden poles weighing about thirty to forty pounds each. About twenty of the slaves in the yard shouldered one, and away they went, merrily singing together. Amongst them was a woman near her confinement, who need not have gone with her companions if she had chosen to remain behind. After breakfast we proceeded to the mine, and on arriving at a place about four miles off we noticed a few of the poles on the ground, but none of the bearers near; our hammock-boys shouted for them, thinking they had perhaps gone into the bush and laid down to sleep, leaving their loads on the road. A woman came out of a thicket and explained that the pregnant woman's time had arrived, and that the child had just been born. Senhor Conceição ordered the women to remain with her till we should arrive at the mine, when he would send bearers with a hammock, blanket, wine, &c., to carry her back. After some time they returned, saying that she and the other women had gone! and when we reached Benguella in the evening, Senhora Conceição described to us her surprise at seeing the women return carrying green boughs, singing merrily, and accompanying the woman bearing her new-born baby in her arms, she having walked back all the way, not caring to wait for the hammock!

An allowance of grog was served out, and a "batuco," or dance, was held by all the slaves in honour of the event, whilst the woman coolly sat on a stone in their midst, nursing her baby as if nothing had happened.

The burial of kings, or head men, and their wives in this part of Angola is very singular. When the person dies, a shallow pit is dug in the floor of the hut in which he or she died, just deep enough to contain the body. This, which is seldom more than skin and bone, is placed naked in the trench on its back, and then covered with a thin layer of earth. On this three fires are lighted and kept burning for a whole moon or month, the hot ashes being constantly spread over the whole grave. At the end of this time, the body is usually sufficiently baked or dried: it is then taken out and placed on its back on an open framework of sticks, and fires kept burning under it till the body is thoroughly smoke-dried. During the whole time the body is being dried, the hut in which the operation is performed is always full of people, the women keeping up a dismal crying day and night, particularly the latter;—I have often been annoyed and had my rest disturbed by their monotonous and unceasing howl on these occasions.

At the pretty town of Lambo I was obliged one night to leave and bivouac at some distance under a baobab, to escape the noise kept up over the dead body of one of the king's wives, which was undergoing the last process of drying over a fire; I looked into the hut and saw a naked bloated body stiff and black on the frame, over a good fire, where, as one of my hammock-boys told me, it would take long in drying, as she was "so fat and made so much dripping." The stench from the body and the number of blacks in the hut was something indescribable.

When the body is completely desiccated it is wrapped in cloth and stuck upright in a corner of the hut, where it remains until it is buried, sometimes two years after. The reason for this is, that all the relations of the deceased must be present at the final ceremony, when the body is wrapped in as many yards of cloth as they can possibly afford, some of the kings being rolled in several hundred yards of different cloth. On the occasion of the burial a "wake" or feast consisting of "batuco," or dancing, with firing of guns and consumption of drink, roast pig, and other food, is held for the whole night.

It is believed that the spirit of the dead person will haunt the town where he died, and commit mischief if the "wake" is not held.

About Ambriz, and on the coast, it is the fashion to place boots or shoes on the feet of free men when they are buried, and old boots and shoes are considered a great gift from the whites for this purpose. The body is generally buried in the same hut occupied by the person during life. In some few places they have a regular burial ground, the graves, generally simple mounds, being ornamented with broken crockery and bottles. The natives have great veneration for their dead, and I found it impossible to obtain a dried body as a specimen, although I offered a high price for one.

Very little ceremony is used in burying blacks found dead, who do not belong to the town in or near which they have died; the wrists and knees are tied together and a pole passed through, and they are then carried by two men and buried outside, anywhere;—if the corpse is that of a man, his staff and "mutete" are laid on the grave; if a woman, a basket is placed on it. (Plate XII.)

Their mourning is simple and inexpensive; a few ground-nuts are roasted in a crock till they are nearly burnt, and being very oily are then readily ground into a perfectly black paste. This, according to the relationship with the deceased, is either rubbed over the whole, or only part of the face and head; in some cases this painting is a complicated affair, being in various devices all over the shaven head and face, and takes some time and pains to effect; and to prevent its being rubbed off at night by the cloth with which they cover themselves, they place a basket kind of mask on their faces. (Plate IV.) This mask is also employed to keep off the cloth from the face and prevent the mosquitoes from biting through.

Circumcision is a universal custom among the blacks of Angola. They have no reason for this custom other than that it would be "fetish" not to perform it, and in some of the tribes they cannot marry without.

The operation is only performed in a certain "moon" (June), the one after the last of the rainy season, and on a number of boys at a time. For this purpose a large barracoon is built, generally on a hill and at some little distance from any town. There the boys live for a "moon" or month under the care of the "fetish man" or doctor, and employ their time in beating drums and singing a wild kind of chant, and in hunting rats in the fields immediately the grass is burnt down. The boys' food is taken up daily by the men of the towns, women not being allowed to approach the barracoon during the time: the path leading to it is marked where it joins the main path by one or two large figures made either of clay or straw, or smaller ones roughly carved of wood, and always of a very indecent character. At the end of the month the boys return to their towns, wearing a head-dress of feathers, singing and beating drums, and preceded by the "fetish man."

Insanity exists, though rarely, among blacks. I have only seen several natural born idiots, but I have been informed by the natives that they have violent madmen amongst them, whom they are obliged to tie up, and sometimes even kill; and I have been assured that some lunatics roam about wild and naked in the forest, living on roots, sometimes entering the towns when hard pressed by hunger, to pick up dirt and garbage, or pull up the mandioca roots in the plantations. This can only be in this part of the country, where the larger carnivora are scarce, or with the exception of the hyena, almost entirely absent.

CHAPTER IX.
CUSTOMS OF THE MUSSURONGO, AMBRIZ, AND MUSHICONGO NEGROES—MANDIOCA PLANT—ITS PREPARATIONS—CHILI PEPPER—BANANAS—RATS—WHITE ANT—NATIVE BEER—STRANGE SOUNDS.

The Mussurongo, Ambriz, and Mushicongo negroes have hardly any industrial or mechanical occupation; they weave no cloths of cotton or other fibre; their only manufactures being the few implements, baskets, pots, &c., required in their agriculture and household operations.

The reason for this want of industry, apart from the inherent laziness and utter dislike of the negroes for work of any kind, is to be found in their socialistic and conservative ideas and laws.

No man can be richer than his neighbour, nor must he acquire his riches by any other than the usual or established means of barter or trade of the natural products of the country, or of his plantations.

Should a native return to his town, after no matter how long an absence, with more than a moderate amount of cloth, beads, &c., as the result of his labour, he is immediately accused of witchcraft or "fetish," and his property distributed among all, and is often fined as well.

I have already mentioned how the natives at Bembe, on receiving their pay, would squander it in riot before leaving for their towns, knowing that it would only be taken away from them, and so preferring to enjoy themselves with it first.

Some of the black traders on the coast, who acquire large values in the ivory trade, have to invest them in slaves, and even form towns consisting of their wives and slaves, and entirely maintained by them;—even these traders are constantly being accused of "fetish," from which they have to clear themselves by heavy payments.

We have already seen how there are hardly any social distinctions among the negroes, and consequently no necessity for finer clothing, food, houses, &c.; it is even considered very mean for one black to eat or drink by himself. Any food or drink, however little, given to them, is always distributed amongst those present. The Portuguese convict whom I have described as owning the sugar-cane plantation at Quincollo, goes under the nickname among the blacks of "Fiadia," or one who eats alone, from his having, when first starting a grog shop, lived in a hut apart, and as the blacks said "when he ate his dinner no other white man saw him, and what was over he kept for the next day."

Nature favours the habits and customs of the blacks, removing all inducement to work by providing with a prodigal hand their few necessities, and exacting scarcely any exertion on their part in return. Their principal food or staff of life, the mandioca root, does not even require harvesting or storing. A knife or matchet, a hoe, a sleeping-mat, and a couple of pots and baskets, enable persons about to marry to begin life and rear a large family without the least misgiving for the future, or anxiety for the payment of rent, doctor's and tailor's bills, schooling, rates, or taxes.

The materials for their huts grow around them in the greatest abundance, a few forked upright poles form the walls, and bear others forming the roof; thin sticks tied horizontally or perpendicularly to the uprights, both inside and out, forming a double wall, complete the framework of the hut, which is then plastered with clay or earth, or covered with grass or "loandos," or mats made of the dried stem of the papyrus. The roof is of grass neatly laid on in layers like thatch, on a frame of light cane or the mid-rib of the palm-leaf. The door is made of slabs of the "Mafumeira" or cotton-wood tree, or of palm-leaves woven together; the door is always about a foot from the ground, and the threshold generally the trunk of a small tree, forming the usual seat of the inmates during the day.

The Mushicongos, living on the mica schist and clay slate formations, which decompose readily, forming tenacious clayey soils, and are the favourite habitat of the white ant, are obliged to prepare with great care the poles employed in building their huts, in order to preserve them from the ravages of that most destructive insect.

For this purpose the poles are soaked for months in stagnant pools, until they become black with fetid mud or slime, and, the end which is intended to be stuck in the ground is then held over a fire till the surface is charred. The smoke from the fire, always kept burning in a hut, preserves it perfectly from the attacks of the white ant, the interior becoming in time perfectly black and shining as if varnished, there being of course no chimney and very seldom a window, though sometimes an open space is left at the top ends for the smoke to issue from.

The furniture is restricted to a bed, made of a framework of sticks or palm-leaves plaited together, and resting on two logs of wood or short forked sticks, so as to raise it about six inches or a foot from the ground. On the bed is laid a sleeping-mat made by the natives of the interior, and sometimes there is a mat-pillow stuffed with wild cotton, but this is seldom more than an inch or two thick;—blacks mostly sleep without pillows, with their heads resting on the extended arm.

The negroes from the interior are sometimes seen using curious small pillows made of wood (Plate IV.) and carved in fanciful patterns; they carry them slung from the shoulder. A very singular habit of all negroes is that of never slinging anything across the shoulders and chest as we do, but always from one shoulder, and hanging under the arm.

Building huts is man's work, and as no nails of any kind are employed in their construction, the sticks only being notched and tied together with baobab fibre, a few days, with but little trouble, suffices to build one.

Women's work is entirely restricted to cultivating the ground and preparing the food. Their simple agricultural operations are all performed with one implement, a single-handed hoe (Plate V.). This hoe is made of iron, nearly round, about the size and shape of a large oyster-shell, and has a short spike which is burnt into the end of the handle, a short knobbed stick about eighteen inches long. With this hoe the ground is cleared of grass and weeds, which are gathered into heaps when dry, and burnt. The ground is then dug to a depth of about six to eight inches, and the loose broken earth scraped together into little hillocks ready for planting the mandioca. This plant, the Cassada or Cassava of the West Indies, &c. (*Manihot aipi*), grows as a peculiar thick round bush from three to six feet high, bearing an abundance of bright green, handsome deeply-cut leaves; it flowers but sparingly, and bears few seeds; it is propagated by cuttings, any part of the stem or branches, which are soft, brittle, and knotty, very readily taking root. About the beginning of the rainy season is the usual time of planting,—two or three short pieces of stem, about a foot long, being stuck in each hillock. In some places two of the pieces are of equal length, and planted near each other, the third piece being shorter, and planted in a slanting position across the other two. This method of planting is supposed, but with what truth I know not, to produce a greater crop of roots than any other. The mandioca is of rapid and luxuriant growth, and in favourable soil the plant throws out many branches. The roots are very similar in outward appearance to those of the dahlia, though of course, very much larger; the usual size is about a foot long, but roots two feet long and several inches wide throughout are of common occurrence. When fresh they are white and of a peculiar compact, dense, brittle texture, more like that of the common chestnut than anything else I can compare it to, and not unlike it in taste, though not so sweet, and more juicy. They are covered by a thin, dark, rough, dry skin, which is very easily detached. Gentle hill-slopes are the places generally chosen for the mandioca plantations, to ensure good drainage, as the roots are said to rot readily in places where water stagnates. The mandioca-root is sufficiently large and good to eat about nine months after planting, but is only pulled up then in case of need, as it does not attain its full perfection for fifteen or eighteen months after the cuttings are planted, and as it can remain in the ground for two or even three years without damage or deterioration, there is no need of a regular time for digging it up. It is eaten fresh and raw as taken out of the ground, though the natives are fondest of its various preparations.

The roots peeled and dried in the sun constitute what is called "bala," and are eaten thus or roasted. "Bombó" is prepared by placing the roots in water for four or five days, running streams being preferred to stagnant pools for this purpose; the outer black skin then peels off very readily and the roots have suffered a kind of acetous fermentation affecting the gluten and gum, and setting free the starch—of which the bulk of the root is composed;— they now have a strong disagreeable acid taste and flavour, but on drying in the sun become beautifully white and nearly tasteless, and so disintegrated as to be readily crushed between the fingers into the finest flour. This "bombó" is also eaten thus dry or roasted, but most usually it is pounded in a wooden mortar and sifted in the "uzanzos" or baskets, into the white flour called "fuba." From this is prepared the "infundi," the food most liked by the natives, which is made in this way:—into an earthen pot half full of water, kept boiling on three stones over a fire, the "fuba" is gradually added, and the whole kept constantly stirred round with a stick; when the mass attains the consistency of soft dough the pot is taken off the fire, and being secured by the woman's toes if she be sitting down, or by her knees if kneeling, it is vigorously stirred with the stick worked by both hands, for some minutes longer, or till it no longer sticks to the side of the pot. Portions of the semi-transparent viscous mass are then transferred with the stick to a small basket or "quinda," dusted with dry "fuba," and rolled round into a flat cake about three or four inches in diameter and a couple of inches thick. It is eaten hot, bits of the sticky cake being pulled out with the fingers and dipped for a flavour into a mess of salt fish, pork, or beans, or into a gravy of stewed mandioca or bean-leaves, Chili pepper, and oil. This "infundi," or "infungi" as it is also pronounced by some of the natives, is delicious eating with "palm-chop."

"Quiquanga" is also a very important preparation of the mandioca-root, large quantities being prepared in the interior and brought down to the coast for sale and for barter for dried fish, salt, &c. The fresh roots are placed in water for a few days, in the same manner as described for "bombó," and peeled, but instead of being dried in the sun, are transferred wet as they are taken out of the water to the wooden mortars, and pounded to a homogeneous paste; this is rolled between the hands into long, flattened cakes about eight inches in length, or into round thick masses. These are rolled neatly in the large, strong smooth leaf of the *Phrynium ramosissimum*—a beautiful trailing plant with a knotted stem, growing very abundantly in moist and shady places,—and steamed over a pot of boiling water carefully covered up to keep the steam in, and then left to dry in the sun or air. The cakes then become fit to keep for a long time, and are of a very close, cheesy, indigestible character, with a disagreeable acid flavour. Cut into thin slices and toasted, the "quiquanga" is not a bad substitute for bread or biscuit.

It is curious that in the district of Loanda and as far south as Mossamedes, the principal food of the people should be a preparation of the mandioca-root, which is hardly ever used by the natives of the country from Ambriz to the River Congo: this is the meal called by the Portuguese and Brazilians "Farinha de pão." It is made by rasping the fresh roots, previously peeled, on a grater, generally a sheet of tin-plate punched with holes or slits, and nailed over a hole in a board. The grated pulp is then put into bags and squeezed in a rude lever-press to extract as much of the juice as possible, and then dried on large round iron or copper sheets fitting on a low circular stone wall, where a wood fire is kept burning. When thoroughly dry it is nearly white, and has the appearance of coarse floury saw-dust, and is excellent eating. Carefully prepared, it appears on all Angolan and Brazilian tables, and is taken dry on the plate to mix with the gravy of stews, &c. Scalded with boiling water, and mixed with a little butter and salt, it is very nice to eat with meat, &c.

Another very favourite way of cooking it is by boiling it to a thick paste with water, tomatoes, Chili pepper, and salt, with the addition of some oil or butter in which onions have been fried. This is called "pirão," and a dish of it appears at table as regularly as potatoes do with us.

With cold meat, fish, &c., it is also eaten raw, moistened with water, oil, vinegar, pepper, and salt, or, better still, with orange or lemon juice, with pepper and salt. This is called "farofa," and is an excellent accompaniment to a cold dinner. The natives generally eat it dry, or slightly moistened with water, and from its being carelessly prepared it is always very gritty with sand and earth, and is the cause of the molars of the natives being always ground very flat. A negro never makes any objection to grit in his food. Fish is always dried on the sandy beach; mandioca-roots or meal, if wet, are also spread on a clean bit of ground and swept up again when dry, and he crunches up his always sandy food with the most perfect indifference, his nervous system not being of a sufficiently delicate character to "set his teeth on edge" during the operation, as it would those of a white man.

Next to the mandioca-root, as an article of food among the blacks, is the small haricot bean; these are of various colours, the ordinary white bean being scarce. A species is much cultivated, not only for the beans, which are very small, but also for its long, thin, fleshy pods, which are excellent in their green state. Beans are boiled in water, with the addition of palm or ground-nut oil or other fat, salt, and Chili pepper. The leaves of the bean, mandioca, or pumpkin plants are sometimes added.

Chili pepper is the universal condiment of the natives of Angola, and it is only one species, with a small pointed fruit about half an inch long, that is used. It grows everywhere in the greatest luxuriance as a fine bush loaded with bunches of the pretty bright green and red berries. It seems to come up spontaneously around the huts and villages, and is not otherwise planted or cultivated. It is eaten either freshly-gathered or after being dried in the sun. It has a most violent hot taste, but the natives consume it in incredible quantities; their stews are generally of a bright-red colour from the quantity of this pepper added, previously ground on a hollow stone with another smaller round one. Their cookery is mostly a vehicle for conveying this Chili pepper, and the "infundi" is dipped into it for a flavour.

Eating such quantities of this hot pepper often affects the action of the heart, and I remember once having to hire a black to carry the load of one of my carriers, who was unable to bear it from strong palpitation of the heart, brought on from the quantity of Chili pepper he had eaten with his food.

In our garden at Bembe we grew some "Malagueta" peppers, a variety with a long pod, and perhaps even hotter than the Chilies. Our doctor's cook, coming to me once for a supply of vegetables, was given a few of these, and commenced eating one. I asked him how he could bear to eat them alone? He laughed, and said he "liked them with rum early in the morning." To try him, I gave him a couple and a glass of strong hollands gin, and he coolly chewed them up and drank the spirit without the slightest indication that he felt the pungency of the fiery mixture. A round and deliciously-scented variety, bearing pods the size of a small marble, is also grown, but is not commonly seen.

Bananas or plantains, grow magnificently, as might be expected, and without requiring the least trouble; yet, such is the stupid indolence of the natives that there is often a scarcity of them. They are principally grown in valleys and other places, where the rich, moist earth in which they delight is found, and where, protected by palm and other trees, they rear their magnificent leaves unbroken by a breath of air. A grove of banana-trees thus growing luxuriantly in a forest clearing is one of the most beautiful sights in nature;—the vast leaves, reflecting the rays of the hot sun from their bright-green surface, contrast vividly with the dark-hued foliage of the trees around, and show off the whorls of flowers with their fleshy, metallic, purple-red envelopes and the great bunches of green and ripe yellow fruit. Numbers of butterflies flit about the cool stems and moist earth, whilst the abundant flowers are surrounded by a busy crowd of bees and other flies, and by lovely sunbirds that, poised on the wing in the air, insert their long curved beaks into the petals in search of the small insects and perhaps honey that constitute their food.

The negroes of Angola always eat the banana raw, but it is roasted by the whites when green, when it becomes quite dry and a good substitute for bread, or boiled, to eat with meat instead of potatoes; and when ripe, roasted whole, or cut lengthways into thin slices and fried in batter and eaten with a little sugar and cinnamon or wine, forming a delicious dish for dessert. A very large plantain, growing as long as eighteen or twenty inches, is cultivated in the interior, and is brought down to the coast by the "Zombos" with their caravans of ivory. Indian corn is the only other plant that is grown and used as food by the negroes of Angola, except the ground-nut already described. It is sparingly cultivated, though bearing most productively, and is eaten in the green state, raw or roasted, and sometimes boiled. About Loanda the dry grain is occasionally pounded into meal and boiled into a stiff paste with water, and eaten in the same manner as the "infundi" from the mandioca-root.

Other edible plants, though not much cultivated by the natives, are the sweet potato; the common yam (which is very rarely seen, and I am quite unable to give a reason for its not being more commonly cultivated); the Cajanus indicus, a shrub bearing yellow pea-like flowers and a pod with a kind of flat pea, which is very good eating when young and green; the purple egg-plant, or "berenjela" of the Portuguese; the "ngilló" (*Solanum sp.*), bearing a round apple-like fruit, used as a vegetable; the ordinary pumpkin, and a species of small gourd; and, lastly, the "quiavo" or "quingombó" (*Abelmoschus esculentus*) of the Brazilians.

The Ambriz and Mushicongo natives make but little use of animal food, seldom killing a domestic animal, and of these the pig is the most esteemed by them. Very little trouble would enable them to rear any quantity of sheep, goats, and other live stock; but, such is their indolence, that, as I have already stated, these animals are quite scarce in the country, and are daily becoming more so.

Blacks, as a rule, seldom engage in the chase. Antelopes, hares, &c., are only occasionally captured or shot, though they are abundant in many places; but they are very fond of field-rats and mice, though house-rats are held in disgust as articles of food. Immediately after the annual grass-burnings the inhabitants of the towns turn out with hoes and little bows and arrows to dig out and hunt the rats and mice. Various devices are also employed to entrap them. A small framework of sticks, about a foot high, is raised across the footpaths, leaving small apertures or openings into which the open ends of long funnel-shaped traps of open flexible wickerwork are inserted. The bushes are then beaten with sticks, and the rats, frightened out of their haunts, rush along the paths into the traps, in which they cannot turn round, and as many as four or five are caught at a time in each (Plate XI.).

Another common trap is made by firmly fixing in the ground one end of a strong stick, and bending down the other end, to which is attached a noose inserted in a small basket-trap, and so arranged as to disengage the bow and catch the unlucky rat round the throat and strangle it as soon as it touches the bait. The rats, as soon as killed, are skewered from head to tail on a long bit of stick, and roasted over a fire in their "jackets" whole, without any cleaning or other preparation, generally five on each skewer.

Frogs are only eaten by the Mushicongos. They are also very fond of grasshoppers, which are beaten down with a flapper, like a battledore, made out of a palm-leaf, their legs and wings pulled off, and roasted in a pot or crock over a fire; they smell exactly like stale dry shrimps.

A large king-cricket (*Brachytrypes achatinus*) is greatly relished everywhere, and the blacks are wonderfully clever at finding the exact spot where one is chirping in the ground, and digging it out from perhaps the depth of a foot or more. It is incredible how puzzling it is to discover the exact place from whence the loud chirp of this insect proceeds.

A large white grub or larva, the interior of which is very streaky in appearance, and which is roasted and eaten spread on a cake of "infundi" as we should spread marrow on a slice of toast, is considered a great delicacy, as also is a very large yellow caterpillar. I have seen, when travelling, all the blacks of my party suddenly rush off with the greatest delight to a shrub covered with these caterpillars, which they eagerly collected to eat in the same way as the grubs I have just described.

The "salalé," or white ant, is eaten by the natives of Angola when it is in its perfect or winged state; they are captured by hand as they issue from holes in the ground, stewed with oil, salt, and Chili pepper, and used as a sauce or gravy with which to eat the "infundi." They have a very sharp taste, from the formic acid contained in them.

The natives of Angola manufacture but one kind of drink, called "uállua" in the district of Ambriz, and "garapa" in the rest of Angola. It is a sort of beer, prepared from Indian corn and "bala," or dry mandioca-root. The Indian corn is first soaked in water for a few days, or until it germinates; it is then taken out and thinly spread on clean banana leaves, and placed on the ground in the shade, where it is left for two or three days; at the end of that time it has become a cake or mass of roots and sprouts; it is then broken up and exposed in the hot sun till it is quite dry, then pounded in wooden mortars and sifted into fine flour; the dry mandioca-roots are also pounded fine and mixed in equal parts with the Indian corn. This mixture is now introduced in certain proportions, into hot water, and boiled until a thick froth or scum rises to the surface. Large earthen pots, called "sangas," are filled with this boiled liquor, which when cold is strained through a closely woven straw bag or cloth, and allowed to stand for one night, when it ferments and is ready for use. It is slightly milky in appearance, and when freshly made is sweetish and not disagreeable in taste, but with the progress of fermentation becomes acid and intoxicating. The rationale of the process of making "garapa" is the same as that of the manufacture of beer. The germination of the Indian corn, in which part of its starch is changed into sugar with the production of diastase, and the arrest of this process by drying, corresponds to the "malting," and the boiling in water with mandioca flour to the "mashing;" the diastase acting on the starch of the mandioca-root, transforms it into sugar, which in its turn is fermented into alcohol, rendering the "garapa" intoxicating, and ultimately becoming acid, or sour, from its passing to the state of acetous fermentation.

The "quindas" or baskets, used by the natives of Angola, are of various sizes and all conical in shape. They are made of straw, but are not woven. A kind of thin rope is made by covering a quantity of straight straws or dry grass stems, about the thickness of an ordinary lead pencil, with a flat grass, or strips of palm leaf, and the basket is built up by twisting this rope round and round, and tightly sewing it together. A coarser kind is made at Loanda for carrying earth or rubbish. It is very curious that no other form of basket should be made in the country, and when a cover is required, another basket inverted is employed.

The "loangos," or "loandos" are large mats about four to five feet long, and from two to four wide; they are made of the dry, straight, flattened stems of the papyrus plant (*Papyrus antiquorum*), and like the baskets are also not woven or plaited, but the stems are passed through or sewn across at several places with fine string made of baobab fibre. These mats are stiff, but at the same time thick and soft; they are used for a variety of useful purposes, such as for fencing, for lying or sitting upon, and for placing on the ground on which to spread roots, corn, &c., to dry in the sun, but principally to line or cover huts and houses. The papyrus grows most luxuriantly in all the pools, marshes, and wet places of Angola, and in many parts lines the banks of the rivers. I have seen it growing everywhere, from a few hundred yards distance from the sea, to as far in the interior as I have been. It is always of the brightest bluish-grey green, and the long, graceful, smooth stalk surmounted by the large feathery head, waving in every breath of wind, makes it a beautiful object. It often covers a large extent of ground in low places, particularly near rivers, to the exclusion of any other plant, and forms then a most lovely cool patch of colour in the landscape, and hides numbers of happy water birds which, unmolested, boom and churrr and tweet in its welcome shade.

Very curious are the sounds that issue in the stillness of the night from these papyrus-covered fields, principally from different species of waterfowl; and I have often remained awake for hours listening to the weird trumpetings, guttural noises and whistlings of all kinds, joined to the croak of frogs and the continual, perfectly metallic, ting, ting, ting—like the ring of thousands of tiny iron hammers on steel anvils—said to be made by a small species of frog.

Nothing gives such an idea of the wonderful multiplicity of bird or insect life in tropical Africa, as the number and variety of sounds to be heard at night. Every square foot of ground or marsh, every tree, bush, or plant, seems to give out a buzz, chirp, or louder noise of some sort. With the first streak of daylight these noises are suddenly hushed, to be quickly succeeded by the various glad notes of the awakened birds, and later on, when the sun's rays are clear and hot, the air is filled with the powerful whirr of the cicads on every tree.

The "uzanzos" are a kind of sieve in the form of an openwork basket, rather prettily and neatly made of the thin and split midrib of the palm leaflets, in which the women sift mandioca, Indian corn, or whatever else they may pound into meal in their wooden mortars. These latter are "uzus," and the long wooden pestles employed with them are termed "muinzus" (Plate XII.).

These mortars are made of soft wood, mostly of the cotton-wood tree, which is easily cut with a knife; for scooping out the interior of the mortars the natives use a tool made by bending round about an inch of the point of an ordinary knife, which they then call a "locombo."

The last article to be described, in daily use amongst the natives of Angola, is a small wooden dish, which is more rarely made now owing to the large quantity of earthenware plates and bowls that have been introduced by the traders on the coast. These dishes are invariably made square in shape (Plate XIV.).

END OF VOL. I.